How I Got Beat-Up by the FBI When I Was Four Years Old

DEE HILL

ISBN: 150242763X
ISBN 13: 9781502427632
Library of Congress Control Number: 2014917255
CreateSpace Independent Publishing Platform
North Charleston, South Carolina

Dad often used to walk around the house wearing only slippers and underwear. And the underwear was usually beat to shit. And whenever Dad walked around the house in those fucked-up undies my mother would get this ironic gleam in her eye and begin to shake her head, a la Deniro, as if to say, "OK, buddy. You wanna play?"

Mom would then walk over to Dad and expose the long, red-painted nail of her right index finger. She would find one of the holes in that Swiss cheesy underwear and slowly tear away. Then she would find a second hole and then a third, repeating the same process until the gravely wounded raiment fell to the ground, vanquished.

Throughout this process I would clap and exclaim, "The Great Zambini!"

When Dad's johnson was finally exposed, he would put on this sad, beaten expression and stumble off to his room, head slumped in mock dejection.

VOICES

I have always heard radio stations in my head. Even if the room I occupy is totally quiet.

Me: "Ma, I always hear voices and music in my head."

Ma: "Me, too. Don't tell your father; he'll get mad."

It was usually the sounds of a deejay droning over some country-western music. Dad liked country-western music.

DAD'S SHIP WAS ALWAYS IN PORT

The ship was always in port at our house. My dad and his navy buddies often spent the night there drinking, playing cards, and watching sports on TV. And starting at the tender age of three, I had to mix the drinks. For example, Dad would go:

"Now mix Jackie's gin and tonic regular the first time, with two fingers like this."

Dad would gesture with his fingers to indicate about two ounces of booze.

I guess the rest of Jackie's drinks were supposed to be weaker…

Or, as Dad put it, "One finger, got it? Jackie is a drunk, and if he misses work, it's your fuckin' fault!"

Of course, I would take a sip from every drink I made to see if it was the right strength. If the drink was too strong and Dad noticed, I would catch a lot of heat. So, I often got a bit tipsy by the time my mother got home from bingo. And every time my mother discovered me a bit tipsy she would scream at my dad. "He's drunk again! They'll take him away from us!"

To which Dad replied, "Good!"

I learned a lot from those lovable, drunken nut bags. I was taught to play poker sitting on their laps. I was taught not to drink too much. Several times I was suddenly hoisted from my perch on the sofa, away from the whisky-perfumed man cave into the bathroom, where the guys had been puking so much that the toilet was clogged and overflowing. Not that anyone noticed as they were all pickled like one of Aunt Milly's prizewinning cukes. These times I was held upside down with the tip of my nose just touching the surface of the cornucopia of barf that was the toilet bowl and was told, "It's OK to drink, but don't be a fuckin' drunken prick like we are!"

Damn fucking straight. And I'll never forget that smell either.

They also made me promise never to get a tattoo. You see, CPO Sully was this great hairy bear of an Irishman who sported a classic green sea horse tattoo on his left forearm. One time, when CPO Sully was all pissy drunk and maudlin, I made the mistake of cuddling up to him.

"What are ya, queer? Fuck off!" snarled Sully.

"I like your tattoo," I countered, impervious to the brush-off.

"I hate tattoos! Never get a tattoo!" He screamed with this possessed look on his mug.

"I hate fuckin' tattoos. I wanna get rid of it. I tried sanding, scraping. It won't never go away! Never get a tattoo!"

Then he started to mock cry and put me into a tight headlock and continued with his rant. "Promise me you'll never get a tattoo. Promise!"

And then Sully clamped my head tighter. All the guys started to laugh and said that I shouldn't mess with Sully when he was depressed.

"I promise! I promise!" was all that I could say. And I never did get a tattoo.

EBONY AND IVORY AND SHIT

I had two friends in high school who formed an interracial couple. Len was a witty, hilarious black kid, and Lonnie was this cute, quiet, white brunette with short hair.

They got on swell. The problem was that Lonnie's dad hated blacks. Her dad had beaten the shit out of her the only two times she brought Len to their house, and he only stopped beating her when she promised not to date Len anymore.

As for Len's family, they were somewhat cool, at best, about the relationship.

"Date a white girl if you have to, but don't bring her around here," said Len's church-going father.

So, this hatred and intolerance of diversity led to some interesting situations. For junior prom, our crew drummed up a beard to pick up Lonnie at her house and pose as her date, pictures and all.

Len and Lonnie also had to get creative as to where they could make out and such. The abandoned fifth floor of the local middle school worked sometimes, when the janitor wouldn't walk in on their sexual escapades and threaten to call their parents. Jealous prick.

Sometimes Len and Lonnie commandeered other people's beds. Like my parents'.

I don't know how many times my dad screamed at me as he held up a used condom." Who's been messing up my bed? The sheets are all soiled! And shit's been left for us to clean up!"

I kept telling Len, "No more holy creamy spermy in my parents' bed."

But they never stopped. Fortunately, we all survived high school. And Len and Lonnie got married, had two beautiful kids, and lived happily, creamily, spermily ever after.

THE OLD SWITCHEROO

I'll have to say that my dad could be pretty cool sometimes, when he wasn't crazy angry.

Junior and senior year he let me keep beer in the old downstairs fridge. But there was a method to his madness. I always kept a few six-packs of good beer like Beck's or St. Pauli Girl in that fridge. But after Dad's fleet pulled in on a Friday, I found that my quality beer had been replaced by Schlitz or some other weasel spoo. Go figure.

Dad was especially cool on the annual navy reserve family day. That fete was usually quite the spectacle. Five year olds, running around drinking cans of beer. OD'ing on hot dogs and brew and sweets and puking their guts out, just like their pops. MPs asking the little shavers who gave them the beer. And when the answer was, "My daddy," the law would say, "Well, that's OK, then."

Then, we would always go down in an old diesel submarine. Those were all painted flat gray inside and had tiny rooms separated by foot-tall thresholds that would be sealed off in case of flooding. We went down about one hundred and fifty feet. And it really felt still and dead quiet down there. I always imagined getting hit with a depth charge and dying in a rusty cat food can at the bottom of the ocean.

HERE WE GO 'ROUND THE ROLLING ROCK

Dad used to get pretty lit up about five or six times a week, always at bars. I guess Dad either hated me and/or Mom, or at least he didn't really like family life. Dad joined the navy at seventeen, during the Korean War, and saw some action in that conflict. And like many young guys who join the military that young, he got caught up in the lifestyle of alcohol, cards, and girls. And like a great many retired military, he could never give up that lifestyle.

As for Dad's navy friends, some of them died in wrecks, some reformed, and some got so sick that they had to reform, sort of.

One time when I was thirteen, Dad took me and two friends, D-Bag and Tito, to the amusement park. Paragon Park to be exact. It featured funky carnival food, like fried dough and fatty hot dogs. The staff was the perfect blend of crazed, dazed carny types who eyed everyone weirdly and displayed bad complexions.

Dad was already pretty wasted before he even picked up my friends. Once we made it to Paragon Park, Dad gave us some Rolling Rock beer to drink. He said the security people would think it was ginger ale, because Rolling Rock comes in a green bottle like ginger ale, and it wasn't sold in Massachusetts yet. And so D-Bag, Tito, and I went off drinking our Rolling Rocks that I carried in a backpack and watched bratty little kids puking up their fried dough and fudge when they got off the roller coaster.

Meanwhile, we began to get pretty tipsy ourselves. Soon we stumbled into this big circus tent that contained a bunch of picnic tables. Out of the corner of my eye, I could see Dad, clearly feeling no pain with a shit-eating grin on his mug, chatting up the biker lady bartender in one corner. The tent featured a high wire that was maybe twelve-feet long and six-feet high. We took the table right underneath the wire. Just then, this old, Eastern European couple stumbled out of a corner with soiled tights and dandruff.

The high-wire act was clearly past it and struggled to make any progress across the twelve-foot distance. At least if they fell, their fall would be broken by landing in my big plate of cheese fries. People were openly laughing. Both performers almost fell twice. To my credit, I was polite, attempting to look on attentively and clapping softly. However, the specter of my polite clapping at this debacle, coupled with way too much Rolling Rock, sent D-Bag and Tito into this wild geyser of laughter. I threw my friends a glance and could not stop chortling myself, so I ran out of the tent, so as not to greatly disconcert the intrepid performers.

But the highlight of the trip came when we left. Dad was as completely blitzed, and his eyes were so completely glazed over that we were sure to experience an adventurous ride home. And what happened is that Dad was so addled by the fermented barley tea that he couldn't find the damn exit. He kept driving around and around the park in a confused haze, just getting madder and madder.

I didn't think much of the situation, as I was pretty tipsy, myself. But then I heard D-Bag blurt out, "He can't find the exit; he's so blotto!"

And then both D-Bag and Tito let out this wild fart of laughter. I was torn between mortification and laughter. Dad either made off that he didn't hear the laughter, or it might have been that he was so used to being shit-faced and hanging out with the guys that in his world it was considered socially acceptable to laugh at fellow drunks who were fucking up badly.

WHAT THE MAID KNEW

In the early eighties, I went to Occidental College in Los Angeles for a year. Small school. Good professors. I had this chubby Latino friend there named Ron, who was obsessed with Diana Ross. He was constantly talking about her records, her concerts, her TV appearances. I didn't mind, because I was a fan of Diana Ross also, and Ron was a fun, kooky guy to hang with. Ron managed to wrangle Diana Ross's home phone number from an acquaintance who was a former employee of hers. Ron quickly called the house and reached the maid. He said the maid was really nice and loved to talk about all aspects of the career of Diana Ross—her concerts, fans, records, etc. The maid told Ron that he could call her up as much as he wanted. I think he called her twice a week for an entire semester. At the end of the semester, wouldn't you know it, the maid confessed that she was actually Diana Ross. And she invited Ron to come to dinner at her mansion in Beverly Hills. Ron was super chuffed, to say the least. I never kept up with Ron after that, because I left Occidental. For all I know, he might have went to work for her. Anyway, there's probably a moral in this tale, somewhere.

AND I THOUGHT THAT I WAS NUTS

I have worked with some crazy, fucked-up people in the one hundred plus shit jobs I have endured. But none have been as Uncle Fuckeluppicus as Lou Bouchet. Lou's life was always this complicated mess of late charges, wage garnishments, cars on the fritz, arrests for failure to appear, and just about any other whacked-out, dysfunctional thing that can turn life into one big hassle. I guess he must have liked it that way, on some level.

One time, Lou was more than an hour late for his shift at Pizza Galore. And it was a really busy day full of snotty liberals. The type of people who say they care so much about their fellow man but really only give a fuck about themselves and their shitty SUVs. (Some nice people, too.)   So, when the line for pizza was halfway around the block, I called up Lou, since his absence was my responsibility, being the deputy vice-assistant manager.

"You are not going to believe this!" began the testimony of Mr. Bouchet. "But I went to this amazing wedding last night. Great time. Open bar. I got so hammered. And get this, I don't know where I am. I'm alone in this house. There's no car in the driveway. I don't know what town I'm in…"

"Can you call a cab, or at least call someone and ask where you are, so you can take a bus?"

"I don't have any money for a bus."

"Can you at least get on a computer and see where you are? Maybe the owner of the pizza shop can pick you up."

"I don't really feel so good. I think I'm gonna lie down. Sorry."

Another time, I called Lou when he was two hours late for work. He said he was under house arrest, wearing an electronic bracelet, and couldn't stray more than fifty feet from his monitor except to go to his primary job at the call center. You can't make this shit up, folks.

HOW I GOT BEAT-UP BY THE FBI WHEN I WAS FOUR YEARS OLD

When I was three, my parents and I lived downstairs in my grandmother's house in Boston. My grandmother lived upstairs. She rented her attic to a skinny Italian-American guy of about twenty-five who looked a lot like Steve Buscemi.

Vince was a nice guy. A little shy and quiet. He usually put up with my incessant demands to play ball or to talk or watch TV. Vince said he was a butcher. Sometimes when he came home from work at ten in the morning, he seemed a bit depressed and withdrawn.

At those withdrawn times, he might punch me in the arm or the stomach if I bugged him to play ball, but I deserved it, because I have always been a pain in the ass.

"I'm sorry, Kid. Don't tell your father, OK?"

"I won't. I'm not a stoolie."

Vince rightly knew that my dad was bat-shit crazy.

So, one night, when my mom and I were hanging out watching TV upstairs at my grandmother's, we heard a loud knock on the front door.

"Open up! FBI!"

I jumped up from the couch and let them in in a jiff. Such a social sort, I am.

Two guys in suits and overcoats, together with two uniformed Boston cops in blue pea coats, quickly entered and got in my grandmother's face.

"We're here to arrest Vincent Perrenti on the charge of homicide," barked one of the agents.

"No! No!" I screamed. "I love Vinny. He's my friend. Don't take Vinny!"

I then got in the faces of the four men and started screaming, "No! No!"

The two Boston cops were pretty nice. But the two FBI agents got really angry.

"If you get in our way, Kid, I'm gonna beat you!"

"I don't care; my dad beats me all the time!"

"Aw, he's just a kid. He doesn't know any better," advised on of the Boston cops.

"If he gets in our way, he's gonna learn real fast not to mess with the law," snapped the agent.

"Don't take Vinny!" I yelled once more before lunging at one leg of each of the two agents who were standing side by side. Immediately one of them started punching and slapping at my arms and legs. It hurt, but I was used to it, as I said. Besides, I wasn't going to give them the satisfaction of hearing me cry in pain. I continued being pounded by both agents for about a full minute. They really did me good, as the Brit hard men would say.

"It's over, Kid. Why are you such a jerk? You are such a jerk," came the voice of Vinny from behind the door to the attic.

"Don't take Vinny!" I yelled once more as Vinny walked calmly through the door and up to the agents to be arrested.

"You're a nice kid, but you're such a jerk," Vinny said, as the Boston cops slapped the cuffs around his wrists. "It's over."

Then the four men led him out of the house.

I was black and blue and in pain for weeks after the incident. Otherwise, the beating had no effect on me. I had no interest in joining the mob, anyway. I took the beating to help a friend.

Vinny spent thirty-three years in the slammer for various murders, but he was let out of prison after it was ruled that the testimony against him was false testimony bought from a lying witness. Vinny was awarded millions by a court and became the godfather of a major crime family.

PADRE PINATA

One day, during my junior year of high school, after the final bell, I was standing at my locker struggling with the beat-up combination lock. I heard a loud crowd of guys coming up behind me. Then someone yelled my name and kicked me hard in the shin.

I whirled around into a karate stance and was about to deliver a blow to the perceived miscreant, when I heard, "Easy!"

I recognized some of my friends and teammates from this mob just milliseconds before I was going to do my best Jackie Chan routine.

"Hey Dee! We're gonna beat the shit out of Father Barnabas. Are you gonna help, or are you gonna be a fuckin' puss?"

"Why do you pussies want to beat the fuck out of that puss?

"Because he's messing with Jackie, that's fuckin' why. You know why. Why are you always fucking with people?"

Jackie was a classmate of ours. A timid, self-effacing kid who worked at the parish rectory two days a week. He was also a teammate of mine on the infamous Bees little league team, whose record of zero wins and twenty losses is still a record. And he peed his pants, too; what an awful fucking smell.

I saw it a little differently between Jackie and Father Barnabus, a fat, forty-ish, greasy, sarcastic prick. I witnessed Jackie and Father Barnabus interacting together in the parish center when we took catechism classes there once a week. Jackie would often come into class to deliver books and supplies. Jackie and

Father Barnabus appeared to be having some kind of playful relationship going on, probably sexual, with lots of pinching and teasing thrown in.

My friends saw things differently.

"I think Jackie and Father Barnabus are having a consensual homosexual relationship. I don't think he's abusing Jackie. Jackie is sixteen. He probably knows what he's doing."

"You and Father Barnabus are having a playful sexual relationship, you mean. Jackie doesn't know his ass from his dildo. He hasn't even kissed a girl yet. And he wets his fuckin' bed, for Christ's fucking sake."

So, the crew took off and beat the fuck out of Father Barnabus. Lots of kicking and stomping, from what I heard. Very Joe Pesci from *Goodfellas*. The crew then went straight to the bishop and read him the riot act: "Eminence, we just beat the fuck out of Father Barnabus for messing with Jackie. You can call the police, but if you do, we're going to the police. Jackie is sixteen."

But the Bishop was like, "No need for that, boys. I'll handle it. I forgive your actions. Boy will be boys."

And so, asshole eminences being asshole eminences, His Assholiness promptly transferred Father Barnabus to Rome. In Rome, Father Barnabus molested a bunch of young Italian kids until one of the parents beat the fuck out of him. Then the bishop there put Father Barnabus on indefinite leave. A few years later, the congressman from our district moved to get Father Barnabus extradited from Italy to face charges of gross cornholing of youth. But His Crappiness, the pope, ruled that Father Barnabus was not a resident of the Vatican, which is a separate country from Italy, and the Italian government wouldn't extradite Father Barnabus, because they said he was in the church, and it was a Vatican affair.

So, go figure.

THE STRAIGHT DOPE AT MR. PHIL'S

Once a week, my mother and her friends would have their beehive hairdos washed and set at Mr. Phil's House of Beauty in Boston. Mr. Phil's was a mob-owned shop, so it didn't really need to make top dollar by cheesing the clientele with cheap décor. The place made good money and treated its customers right. Nice carpeting, free espresso, and yummy Italian pastries.

The ladies would spend half the day there. I loved it for both the food and the drama. The wise guys would come in one by one. They would enjoy a cappuccino and an éclair, flirt a bit with the older ladies, and then chat with Phil about things. It was very casual, and everyone was in the know. Of course, sometimes Phil would show up with a cast on his arm or a black eye and no explanation. Everyone just figured Phil couldn't make the vig for the month.

Phil was very sweet but could also be quite bitchy at times. He would always personally mix my coffee drink special, with one shot of espresso and like sixteen ounces of steamed milk with sugar. I can still hear Phil asking attentively, "What's it gonna be today, Kid? We got macaroons, but they're a little stale. The pizzelles are still good. Oh! I didn't even see the biscotti."

One time, Phil came out of his office arm in arm with this tall, hunky, blond guy. The old biddy clientele was very casual, even though there were a lot of little kids in the shop. My mother's friend, Phyllis, a chain-smoking freak, would always be the one to clue me in to shit. She would put her arm around my neck, move in conspiratorially, and say like Cagney, "Some guys like guys. Deal with it,

Kid." Phyllis would then take a couple of deep, quick drags of her cigarette and blow a huge cloud of smoke in my face for emphasis.

Or maybe Phil had just broken up with someone and would be on this crying jag.

"He's such a bitch. I gave him everything!"

To which some Italian granny would be like, "You're too good for him, Phil," or "He was all wrong for you, anyway. Why don't you meet a nice Italian boy?"

Needless to say, it's not quite the same experience when we go to Cost Suckers for a seventeen-dollar bowl cut.

SALE OF THE CENTURY

In high school, the editor of the school newspaper and president of the drama club was a chubby, hairy lounge lizard named Lou Seahorn. In addition to these artistic endeavors, Lou was also the school's biggest drug dealer.

One time, Lou's hippie mom began her once-a-year cleaning of their house and happened upon this huge stash in Lou's room. In each corner of the room was a chest of drawers. Every drawer of each chest was crammed with baggies of marijuana, Thai sticks, hash, opium, sinsemilla, valium, bennies…everything except heroin. At first sight of this cornucopia of seventies excess, Lou's mom declared that he had to get rid of the drugs by the end of the month or leave the house. So, what was Lou to do but break into the Xerox room of Gulchwater-Grimwald Regional High and print up eight hundred four-page flyers: "Lou Seahorn's Going Out of Business Drug Sale." Some of the highlights included opium at seven dollars a gram and speed at fifty cents a hit.

Anyway, lots of students were walking around the school openly looking at this price list. It's amazing no one got in trouble over it. I remember sitting right next to the open door in Miss Grey's writing glass, ogling the teacher's tight white jeans that were tucked into red spike-heeled leather boots, when I saw one of the biggest stoners in the school stumbling in the hall: a beautiful, tall brunette named Jill. She immediately walked up close to me and yelled very loudly, "Do you know where I can buy any speed?"

I immediately whipped out my Lou Seahorn Going of Business Drug Sale flyer and showed it to her.

"Lou has a sale on hits of speed for fifty cents!" I yelled. Miss Grey just laughed, because it was the seventies, and even Jesus Christ was getting high and partying.

These days, we would have had the SWAT team in and the psychiatrist and the counselors and that bitch from social services.

Anyway, Lou finally sold his whole stash for forty cents on the dollar to the high school motorcycle gang, which consisted mostly of a bunch of effeminate poofs who smoked clove cigarettes and wore octagon-shaped glasses.

At this point, I will share a recipe: Beef Penang Curry.

The only books that sell these days are those concerning sex, religion, self-help, and food, so I will try to include as many of these crowd pleasers as possible.

Beef Penang Curry

Ingredients:

1 pound top sirloin or flank steak (thinly sliced)

1 cup of peas

1 tablespoon Penang curry (available at your local bizarre foreign food shop)

1 tablespoon fish sauce

1 teaspoon sugar

15/16 ounces of good-quality, thick coconut milk (not the cheapo crap)

1 tablespoon canola oil

Directions:

Place tablespoon of oil in wok. Heat wok until oil is hot.

Add a tablespoon of Penang curry paste. Let paste and oil heat up and become fragrant. Stir the mixture up a bit.

While the mixture is getting fragrant (a few minutes), mix the fish sauce and the sugar in with the coconut milk in the can.

Add the meat, and cook till half done. Add the coconut milk mixture. Cook for five minutes.

Add the peas. Cook for five more minutes.

Serve with white or brown rice.

HOLY UFO, BATMAN!

Mr. Russell was a very sober and well-respected fifth-grade science teacher. He had twenty-nine years in the school system and was nearing retirement. One day in his class, I found myself getting a bit bored with Mr. Russell having to explain the concept of aeration for the fifth time to all the yo-yos in the back. I vaguely heard him remonstrate with one of the students for not doing his homework as I feasted on the sight of Sally Imperara's long, silky, brown hair and her purple velvet hot pants and jacket with white vinyl go-go boots.

"Listen up!" said Mr. Russell, louder than usual. He then took off his thick black glasses and eyed us all very seriously. "Let me tell you something. I have a friend who has been a pilot with the air force for twenty years. In the early sixties, he was ordered to get in his plane and follow a flying saucer. When he got close to it, the saucer reversed direction and took off at about three thousand miles per hour. My friend asked his commander if the flying saucer could be ours or the Soviets. Negative was the answer."

Mr. Russell then looked into the eyes of each one of us and advised, "Don't let anyone tell you otherwise. This UFO shit is for real, and there are people from other planets visiting us. Sorry for swearing. Now, where were we?"

Another UFO story comes to mind. One time my parents went out and left my cousin, Tony, to babysit me. When my parents were saying goodbye, the *Smokey Bear Show* was on TV. When my parents left, Cousin Tony abruptly turned off the set, announcing, "Fuck this Smokey the Bear shit. We're gonna listen to something really interesting while the old squares are gone."

THE UFO EXPERIENCE PART II

Tony turned on the radio to some nighttime talk show. The guest was Jesse Marcel. I guess he was one of the intelligence officers at Area 51 in 1947 when an alleged UFO crashed in New Mexico. Mr. Marcel talked about seeing mangled alien bodies. My cousin's eyes lit up at this testimony, and he started yelling at me like a carnival barker.

"So, what ya think about that, young man?"

I said that I thought it was interesting, but it didn't really rock my world. For one thing, I had watched enough of the *Lost in Space* TV show that aliens didn't seem that weird. That's probably why they produced such a show in the first place. Secondly, what really rocked my world was getting hit and yelled at all the time by my parents. Nothing else came close to being that upsetting. And nothing else will ever come that close. Furthermore, I had this sneaking suspicion that if the aliens became a part of our human society, they would be conservative and do stuff like buy McDonald's franchises. I can see myself paying for my two value menu double cheeseburgers, saying to the owner working the register, "What up, Meepzor? How come the Rockies are always so crappy?"

"The owners are too poor to compete, man. That's two dollars and sixty-seven cents, please," the gray alien in the McDonald's uniform would say, smiling.

DRIVEN BY MRS. WASHINGTON

In sixth grade we had this black, middle-aged reading teacher named Mrs. Washington. She had a wry sense of humor, but she was also very detached and clinical. Whenever a student would act out in class, Mrs. Washington would announce, "Gene does not like himself today." And then she would ask, "Gene, why do you not like yourself?"

All of us would crack up and wonder, what the fuck? But Mrs. Washington would continue with the sweetest smile. "Gene, if you continue to not like yourself perhaps you should seek some therapy."

Gene would laugh and say that what he didn't like was the class, but Mrs. Washington was on a roll:

"Gene, if the cost of therapy is a problem, I know of many programs that offer counseling at no cost."

Heavy shit. If there had been a rat line from the reeducation camps of the Soviet Union, as there had been with the Nazis after World War II, I would have had a better idea of where Mrs. Washington had come from.

We did manage some payback against the account of Mrs. W. I remember that we did the same book report five or six times on this inane book called *Leave It to Herbert the Electrical Mouse*. It was about a suburban family's pet mouse that was given its walking papers by his mama-san. However, by the end of the book, the mouse, Herbert, redeems himself by alerting everyone to a loose electrical cable located behind a wall. Either Mrs. Washington didn't give a shit that we gave the same book report half a dozen times, or she was so up in the clouds with her communist new world order newspeak that she didn't notice.

Ironically, I did learn a lot in Mrs. Washington's class about black American history. I learned about the Reconstruction Era, Bethune-Cookman, Harriet Tubman, Crispus Attucks, and John Drew. I never knew that John Drew discovered plasma. And I had never heard that he died after a severe accident, because he was refused admittance to the nearby white hospital.

One time, Gene asked Mrs. Washington why it was always "Black History Day" in her class. Mrs. Washington said that she focused on black history because there was no black history being taught at this middle school, and there we no black teachers beside herself in this middle school, and there were very few black people in the town we lived in. Fair enough.

Further, Mrs. Washington told Gene that when he started to like himself perhaps he would start to appreciate the history of other cultures.

Tou-fucking-ché.

THE MOB AND ME

The father of Gino and Tommy, my friends next door, ran a bakery downtown in Medford in the midsixties. Mr. Torani made such yummy pastries. Cannoli with rum cheese filling, pizzelle cookies with anisette flavor, and macaroon cookies.

Mr. Torani was also a bookie for the mob, so the boys were seen filing in regularly at the bakery to check on tings. The guys always wore very sharp suits with cool accessories like gold lighters and watches. The two Torani kids (resembling Steve Buscemi and Nicholas Cage) and I were always hanging out at one of the two bakery tables, doing serious damage to the chocolate éclairs and Italian nougat.

"Just the day-old stuff, Madonna! You guys are gonna put me outta business!" said Mr. Torani on a daily basis.

The wise guys were always polite and generous to us kids.

"Are you guys being good boys?"

"Yes, Mr. Tutterelli," we would always say in unison. And to complete the daily ritual, Mr. Tutterelli or Mr. Lupi or Mr. Garafalo, whomever it was that day, would give us each a couple of dollars or even a five.

"Thank you, Mr. Digentamastroaintino!"

Gotta love some of these Italian names. As for the money, I didn't tell my dad, because he would get mad. My mother is Italian-American. She digs gangsters. Dad would have gone ballistic if he knew. So, I spent the money quietly on candy and baseball cards. I saved all my baseball cards, too. But just when I was about to sell them in the 1990s, they got stolen. Ten thousand in collectables gone—kapluey!

Actually, I just confessed to my mom last week (at the age of fifty-two) that the wise guys were giving me money. She just laughed.

One of my mom's cousins was also in the mob. One time at a BBQ at that cousin's house, I politely asked Cousin Frank why he got into his business. Frank eyed me up and down and said, "When you're forty, you'll understand. And then maybe you'll give me a call."

I'm over forty now. I understand. But I haven't given him the call, yet.

As it turns out, even my sweet great uncle Sal, a brother of my grandmother, had been in the mob, too. A leg-breaker. I learned that information when my sister had been having trouble with her prick husband roughing her up.

"Why don't you have your mob relative rough up this asshole?"

I asked my mom.

"Which one? Frank or Sal?"

"Uncle Sal was in the mob? He seemed like a nice old man who was always trying to restore his old Stanley Steamer."

"Get with it, Sister!" said Ma in her best Cagney imitation.

As a little kid in the late thirties, my mother loved going to the Warner Bros. gangster pictures. And she always talked like George Raft, endlessly going on about hot tickets and things being on the up-and-up or on the QT.

I had another cousin who was briefly in the mob, but he was killed at the age of twenty-two in a mob war. The wake was closed casket, as he had been shot up very badly. The highlight of the wake was when one of his seventy-year-old uncles knelt by the casket and started screaming, "I'm gonna get you mother-fucking cocksuckers!"

SPIRITED HIJINKS IN THE GREAT OUTDOORS

I was never in the Boy Scouts. Camping has never appealed to me, nor did the merit badge activities. I always preferred sports as a kid.

When our local scout troop took camping trips, Mr. Bonaduce, the scout master, would spend the whole trip holed up in his tent listening to the Red Sox on the radio and getting hammered on vodka. Meanwhile, the tender young scouts were experimenting with drugs and homosexuality. Eventually the national Boy Scout office found out about these spirited hijinks and suspended our town chapter for ten years.

The star of the festivities was this retarded kid named Sucky Chucky. Evidently, he was giving blow jobs to all comers.

EXOTIC FLORA AND FAUNA

One kid in our high school was especially unusual. His name was Frederick. He had really thick black hair and wore thick black glasses. He was short, walked in a hunched-over fashion, and always seemed to be wearing a bright orange parka. Whenever we had to do some oral report or some project, Frederick would produce some whacked-out lulu. One time we had to do this report on a region of France for über-uptight sunt Madame Crevier's French class. So, what did Frederick do? Well, he borrowed an eight-millimeter Laurel and Hardy film from the town library and projected that onto a classroom wall. Frederick then played an audio tape of a toilet flushing.

Everyone was like, "What the fuck?" But I thought it was a brilliant comedic take on the ineffectuality of French foreign policy, especially in the light of their constant criticism of their American counterparts. And I said as much. However, Madame Crevier just gave me a dirty look and promptly sent Frederick to the school psychiatrist, Dr. Lamont.

Later that year, Lenny saw Frederick in the boy's locker room after school hours lying on the floor with Sucky Chucky doing a sixty-nine. Phil asked what they were doing, and Frederick said they were drawing on the infinite power of the universe.

After high school graduation, Frederick moved down the street from Stephen King in Maine. Frederick washed dishes at a restaurant and then wrote science fiction stories all night. According to a mutual friend, Frederick would bang on King's front door every evening and yell, "Mr. King! Mr. King! Will you read my science fiction stories!"

I heard that Mr. King was very nice to Frederick and read his stories several times. King's verdict was that the stories were pretty interesting but needed more character development. Years later, in the book *Pet Cemetery*, there is an unkempt character, with thick black hair and thick glasses, who walks all hunched over. So, now you all know where that guy came from.

BRIDGE OVER THE RIVER SHRINK

I was first sent to Dr. Lamont by Madame Crevier. One time she made us do a family tree on poster board. I didn't feel like doing the project, so I just played it for laughs. I included a picture of Burt Reynolds posing in his undies as my uncle and a picture of *Star Trek*'s Lieutenant Uhura as my aunt. The gang laughed, but Madame Crevier said that I was ill and needed to have my head examined. So, off I went to Dr. Lamont.

Dr. Lamont was this hip, black cat of about fifty. I hate it when people automatically associate the words "hip" and "black," because most people aren't that cool. But Dr. L was very cool.

When I showed the poster board family tree to Dr. Lamont, he almost fell off the desk he was sitting on he was laughing so hard.

"Whew! Ha! That's funny stuff, man. But you must realize that Madame Crevier is pretty uptight, so maybe play it a little more serious with her next project, all right? That woman is always sending her students down here to me for no reason. My professional opinion is that woman needs some therapy."

Well, the first thing I did when I got back to class was to proclaim loudly, "Dr. Lamont said you need to have your head examined."

"Oh, he did, did he?"

And off went Madame Crevier to see Dr. Lamont. Madcap laughter from the gang for the whole five minutes that the teacher was gone. When Madame Crevier returned, she stared me down and sent me back for round two with Dr. Lamont. When I got to the school psychologist's office, Dr. Lamont was like, "Will everyone just please cool it? What is wrong with all of you?"

GEE MISTER, YOUR GARDEN GNOME SURE IS FEISTY

Mr. Potemkin was another teacher who was always sending kids to see Dr. Lamont. Mr. Potemkin was a short, fat, balding, and belligerent guy who wore thick glasses. He was always threatening to give everyone thirty days detention, too.

Mr. Potemkin was a decent lecturer and made medieval European history fairly interesting. But what was more interesting was the many ways that Mr. P would freak-out after someone pissed him off. One time we had to do this very involved timeline of Russian history on poster board. I spent about eight hours on it, and it looked pretty good.

"Is this piece of crap the best you can do? Wait until you get into the army!" Snarled Mr. P.

"Have you ever been in the army?" I countered.

"No."

"That's because you were too short to reach the urinals."

Loud laughter from the gang. Visit number three to Dr. Lamont. This time, Dr. Lamont was like, "You gotta realize, man, that you're a lot smarter than most of these teachers, and it makes them really uptight. So, can you cool it?"

"But this guy is such a jerk; can't they fire him and get someone else?"

"If we do that, we'll just end up with someone worse."

Another time Dr. P interrogated everyone about what they wanted to do with their lives. When he got to Frederick, God love him, that nut bag, in all seriousness, said that he was going to take a command post with a secret otherworldly regime to defend human civilization against a nascent alien invasion.

Mr. P then stared at me and asked me what I thought of Frederick's plans. I said that they were very provocative. Mr. P stared into space for a full minute.

"I am provoked. Yes. I am very provoked. Master Frederick, I sentence you to a session with Dr. Lamont. Now!"

Exeunt Frederick.

LITTLE WOP, BIG APPALACHIANS

My Dad's side of the family lived in North Carolina. Very warm and witty people. I loved the closeness of the neighbors. At lunchtime, maybe twelve family members would sit down to a hearty lunch of ham, collard greens, lima beans, homemade biscuits, gravy, and blackberry pie. Then some neighbors would start showing up during the meal. They would let themselves in through the unlocked door, grab a plate of food, and dig in for a bit before they would start saying hello. Very casual.

Whenever someone would ask one of my many uncles for a favor, they would all do some hilarious, dumb Southerner routine that could last ten minutes. Very *Amos 'n' Andy* or Two Black Crows. Of course, they would always gladly do the favor afterward.

One time we traveled east to the Appalachian Mountains area of North Carolina and visited some second cousins who lived in twenty-by-eighteen-foot wooden shacks.

I didn't care what they lived in, but the patriarchs of those families were very tough and mean looking and eyeballed me severely to see if I showed the slightest trace of condescension.

We then all went to a picnic area and watched a jug band. An amazing jug band.

Picture this scene. My hillbilly family in overalls and slouchy hats sitting on blankets around a porch that was torchlit. Around them sat about one hundred other hillbillies with overalls and slouchy hats. Sitting with my family was me, a fat Italian-looking kid in a striped shirt.

The band stood on the porch. There was a banjo player, a jug player, and a guy playing a piece of string tied to a broomstick. They played with great passion and skill. And they looked serious. And they looked mean. And the whole hour that they played they stared at me, hard. They were all staring at me so hard I just knew that after the show one of them was gonna beat me up. But I was used to it. So, I just enjoyed the show and figured I would take my lumps afterward.

And wouldn't you know it, at the end of the show, right after the applause died down, the banjo player lunged at me quick as a cat and grabbed me. He carried me up to the other band members and hugged me as the crowd shrieked, and one old man said, "Son, never forget this moment; that's Stringbean."

Stringbean turned out to be just a sweet as he was tough looking.

"I bet you think we're just a bunch of dumb hicks," he said.

"No! You guys are great," I countered quickly, neither wanting to hurt the feelings of others or get my head hurt.

"And what is someone that looks like you doin' in the Appalachian Mountains watching a jug band in the middle of nowhere?" asked the banjo player. A reasonable question as I resembled that fat Italian kid, Anthony Martinetti, who was featured in the spaghetti commercial in the sixties, where his mother is yelling, "Anthony! Anthony! Time for supper."

"I'm with my family," I explained.

"Your family. Well, where is your family? Show me."

I pointed to my hillbilly relatives. The banjo player looked and wasn't convinced.

"That ain't yer family."

"Is too."

"Show me your mama."

I pointed to my mother, who resembles Rene Taylor, who portrayed the mother of Fran Drescher in *The Nanny*.

"Now I get it," reasoned Stringbean. He then showed me a few chords on his banjo in a very sweet and kind and loving manner. I was then seized by the jug player, who also gave me the same interrogation.

"I bet you think we're just a bunch of dumb hillbillies."

"I do not. My dad's family lives here."

"Show me yer family."

After this second third degree was over, the jug player explained that he used several different jugs with different amounts of liquid in each to get a different note. He was a very kind and sweet person. He let me blow on the different jugs to see the different notes that came out of them. Good fun.

All in all, it was a very memorable evening.

RELIGIOUS INTERLUDE.

Since religious books also sell, I include this religious interlude to cover this particular base.

One of my cousins in North Carolina was a Baptist preacher at the Church of Hellfire and Eternal Damnation. I always caught his services when I was in North Carolina. The last time I caught his act, he really was on fire. He related this hellish dream to the faithful:

"Last night I had a terrible dream! Just Terrible! Want to know what it was?"

"Amen! Amen! Tell us!" screamed the faithful.

"I dreamed that I had died and gone to hell!"

"No!" and "Not that!" came the screaming replies from the faithful.

"I saw the fires of hell, and I heard the most terrible screams that you can imagine. And I saw a man on fire, the skin peeling of his body, writhing in the most intense pain! And the man saw me. And when I turned to him, he started to yell, 'Almost! Almost! I almost made it to the Kingdom of Heaven. I went to church every Sunday! I read my Bible, but I never got around to practicing what I learned. I almost did. Almost! Almost! Almost!' So, my parishioners, if you are like this man and have *almost* begun to act in a Christian manner and live a life according to scripture, I suggest you start today, because you never know when your hour will be up!"

"Amen!" and "That's right!" came the reply from the faithful.

I wanted to tell my cousin that if his God was that ornery, he should fire that God and get one more simpatico. But he just would have laughed.

Another religious story concerns my grandmother. One summer I asked my grandmother how come there was a Baptist church in town for white people and another one for black people. My grandmother laughed and said that white people and black people worship differently. She said that black folk make a lot of noise in church, while white people like a quieter service.

This reminds me of the times we were invited over to eat with my grandparents' neighbors, the Lincolns, who lived at the next farm about half a mile away. Whenever my mom and dad and I left the my grandparents' house to dine with the Lincolns, my grandmother would declare, "Now you have to be careful with the food at the Lincolns. It's really good food, but it's very rich. Mrs. Lincoln makes that black soul food, so eat it slowly."

Now, the food grandma cooked was fatback, corn bread, collard greens, fried chicken, fried squirrel, chicken and dumplings, homemade biscuits, apple pie, pecan pie, blackberry pie, persimmon pudding, etc. The food that Mrs. Lincoln made was fatback, corn bread, collard greens, fried chicken, fried squirrel, chicken and dumplings, homemade biscuits, apple pie, pecan pie, blackberry pie, persimmon pudding, etc.

So, one time I said to Grandma all wide-eyed, "Grandma! You make soul food, too."

Well, Grandma just laughed like mad. And so did the rest of my family.

"White people don't make soul food," said Grandma.

"But you do! You do make soul food, Grandma!"

Aunt Clem is the biggest character out of my Southern relatives. Recently, she was pulled over by police for driving over one hundred miles per hour in downtown Raleigh, North Carolina. Evidently, Aunt Clem had pulled up to a group of Mexican kids in a hot rod at a red light just outside of town and yelled, "You guys ain't got nothin'!" Aunt Clem then blew the doors off their hot rod with her souped-up Acura.

In the old days, before police radios, Aunt Clem and Uncle Jimmy used to lead police cars on high-speed chases all over the South. Very *Dukes of Hazard*. But according to Aunt Clem, it wasn't their fault. Evidently, in rural towns in the South in the forties, if you refused to buy oil for your car in a gas station, the sheriff would find a way to ticket you. This was the only means of revenue for some of these small towns. Well, Aunt Clem and Uncle Jimmy would have none of that.

Aunt Clem also possesses about twenty-three guns of various types. I know that because I called her at work and asked to borrow a gun. She said to go into the towel drawer in her room and pick one out. Well, what a cornucopia of excess I found. Glocks, Berettas, .22 revolvers, .22 pistols, 357s, and .44s.

I am just a mediocre shot, myself. Even though Dad first put a .22 revolver in my hand and told me to shoot at the tender age of eight.

But the weirdest thing that ever happened in the South took place when I was three years old. I had just learned to use the men's room all by myself. Before that, my mom took me to the lady's room. I was told to go into the bathroom and look for the urinal, and then I would know it was the men's room, as I could not yet read. Well, one time in rural North Carolina, I had to go to the bathroom at some rest stop. My dad was busy chatting with my uncles as I wandered into one of the bathrooms. Finding the urinals, I immediately started to pee. But when I came out of the bathroom, Dad was really pissed off.

"What's wrong, Dad?" I asked.

"You took a piss in the wrong bathroom. That's what's wrong!"

"But I was in the men's room. I saw the urinal."

"But that's the black men's bathroom! Can't you fucking read?"

"But I can't read, Dad. And how come there are two different men's rooms? One for blacks and one for whites? That doesn't make sense."

Before Dad could open his mouth and yell again, this big black dude comes up to dad and gets in his face and says very loudly, "Yeah, how come there's two bathrooms? One for blacks and one for whites. Don't make sense."

Dad just walked away, because this dude was really big.

DISCO INFERNO AT MISS ANZALONE'S TENTH GRADE ENGLISH CLASS

It could also get pretty musical up north in high school during the disco era. In class, during tenth grade, whenever anyone would mention the words "brick," "house," "slippery," or "wet," several of my friends would start a disco line dance and sing either "Slippery When Wet" or "Brick House" by the Commodores. I can still hear them now: "She's a brick…hoooouuuuuuse!"

The teachers were very cool and just laughed. Even though the dance routine could last for three or four minutes. Very fun. Very Caz. Very Seventies.

No police. No SWAT teams. No bitch from social services.

IDI AMIN AND ME

In the Latin class sophomore year, the teacher, Mr. Gaspari, got all of us students hooked on the BBC series *I, Claudius*. In this series, a couple of the Roman emperors behaved outrageously. Especially Caligula, who was emperor just before Claudius.

Caligula turned his palace into a brothel and pimped out all the senators' wives. He also got his sister pregnant. He then proclaimed himself to be a god.

At first I was freaked-out by this behavior. But then I said, "Wait a minute!" I realized that if I ever possessed absolute power, I would act in much the same way. Especially the part where he proclaims himself a god.

I guess that's why I was such a big fan of Idi Amin Dada, the president for life of Uganda. Everyone was saying that Amin was a madman, because he fed hundreds of his enemies to the crocodiles, but like I said, I would feed my enemies to the crocodiles if it was legal and if I had any enemies.

And wouldn't you know it, later that year I was elected head of the World Affairs Club at school. And that power meant that I could choose which small country to represent at the Washington, DC, Model UN that year. Colleges like Harvard and Yale sent teams to this UN, and they represented the big and powerful countries.

So, which country did I pick? You know the answer: Uganda. And it wasn't a month later that our World Affairs Club advisor, Mr. Gaspari, came in to

Madame Crevier's French class and said that the Ugandan Cultural Ministry was on the phone. He wanted to ask me why I picked Uganda to represent at the Model UN. I told the minister that if I ruled a country, I would run it exactly as President Amin did. And I would, too. The cultural minister then told me Amin asked him to invite our delegation to lunch when we got to Washington for the Model UN.

Ironically, Mr. Gaspari intercepted me in the hallway a month later and said that the cultural minister wouldn't be having lunch with us, because he had just been fed to the crocodiles by Idi Amin, and Mr. Gaspari said that he hoped I was satisfied.

EPIC BATTLE

One time in high school, my friends and acquaintances took part in a rumble with another town. It was all over Danny Mooney. Danny Mooney was this wet noodle of a guy I really didn't give a shit about. Mooney worked at the bowling alley downtown. It seems that there were some young guys from Middleboro (a neighboring town) acting out in the bowling alley one night. When Mooney told them to leave, they slapped him around a bit. No big deal. But a lot of our guys took offense. What's more, a lot of our guys knew some of the Middleboro guys. And words were exchanged, along with foul oaths. And the next thing you know, my friends are asking me to take part in a rumble with Middleboro that afternoon after school. It was supposed to be about fifty against fifty. No knives or guns, but chains and baseball bats were OK.

Ex-fucking-scuse me? I'm supposed to get my head bashed in for Danny Fucking Mooney? Fuck Danny Fucking Mooney!

"It's also for the honor of our town."

"Fuck our town. It has no honor. It's a bunch of fat freaks like me OD'ing on junk food."

So, my friends and acquaintances met the Middleboro host on our town common and routed them completely. A few Middleboro guys suffered concussions when a few of our guys hit them over the heads with baseball bats. I wouldn't mess with our guys—generally a lot of crazy bastards.

I would file the whole fiasco under O, either for "Oy-vay!" or "Oh, dear!"

TRIBUTE TO A GOOD GUY

When I was a little kid growing up in Massachusetts in the midsixties, there was a neat old kid in the neighborhood, maybe fifteen, named Jeff. He was always doing cool stuff. Riding minibikes, fixing up go-carts, and working on the many stylish cars he picked up cheaply at the small junkyard on the corner of our street on Bowen Avenue.

Jeff was really cool with all the little kids in the neighborhood. This was an Italian-American neighborhood, so there were always lots of noisy little kids hanging around and playing stickball, Wiffleball, touch football, or just generally annoying the shit out of everyone.

In short, we were often a pain in the ass. However, Jeff usually had time for us kids. He'd show us how to change the oil in a car or how to clean the spark-plug on a lawnmower. He was always smiling and helpful to everyone. We would often see him helping older ladies to cross the street or unloading their groceries. Jeff was the real deal. He was not some Eddie Haskell type of character who was trying to score points with Jesus or some shit like that.

Jeff's dad, Mr. V, was also really cool with the neighborhood kids. Mr. V. was always doing things like showing kids how to ride a minibike safely. Always smiling and sweet to everyone.

As Jeff approached the age of eighteen, he talked of joining the air force and learning to fly airplanes, but then a good friend of Jeff's was killed in the Vietnam War. In the spirit of revenge, Jeff joined the army. I don't think Jeff had been in Vietnam for more than a month when news arrived to Medford that Jeff had been killed in a firefight.

How could life suck that badly? I felt like I had trouble breathing. I'll never forget how much Mr. V. cried. He cried for months. Loudly. I could hear him from three houses over. He walked the neighborhood in a daze. And if you said hello to him, he would say, "Fuck you."

I still don't know what to make of that, except that life often motherfucking sucks.

It's funny. I hadn't thought of Jeff for decades until the news became so full of right-wing chicken hawks who always want others to fight in wars but weaseled out of military service. People like Bill O'Reilly of Fox News. And Rush Limbaugh.

I am middle of the road politically, and like Jeff, I think that the United States is a swell place to live, but I wish we would tune out these TV warriors and concentrate on making this country rich again.

ERNEST AND JULIO GALLO: EAT YOUR HEART OUT

I had this one crazy friend in high school named D-Bag. He was a great drummer as well as an unredeemable klepto and scam artist. D-Bag was always on the make with the schemes and the women. He lived with his sweet, long-suffering mom and his surly, alky stepdad in this four-story maze-like former convent.

One time in seventh grade, D-Bag made a batch of wine from a bottle of Welch's grape juice and some yeast. It was OK wine but a bit too sweet. We drank about half of it and stored the rest in the seldom-occupied doghouse of D-Bag's whacked-out pooch, Clarkie. Clarkie had the body of a miniature poodle, the head of a German shepherd, and the personality of a crocodile. Clarkie ended up biting everyone. He even bit D-Bag's sweet old grandma. If you think there's a loving, caring God, reflect upon Clarkie for a moment.

When we went to Clarkie's doghouse a few days later to finish off the batch, we found D-Bag's dad sitting in a lawn chair, sipping the wine as he wore a floppy sun hat and a silly shit-eating grin.

"You kids are still wet behind the ears! Why don't you get a job?" teased Mr. G in careless alcoholic bliss.

So much for that day's buzz. But I consoled myself with the thought that even though Mr. G was stepping on our high, at least the wine was helping him ease off the hard stuff. Mr. G had been a solid quart-a-day man in the vodka department for the many years I had known him.

Also, for a while in seventh and eighth grade, D-Bag and I would make some extra money by getting his kooky, cool, older brother Ben to buy bottles of Boone's Farm wine for eighty-nine cents. We would then sell the wine to friends at four dollars per bottle. A nice little money-maker, really.

Ben had just washed-out from a few months in the coast guard and was doing odd jobs like mowing lawns and corrupting young kids. Usually we could tempt Ben away from his Hendrix LPs and *Monty Python's Flying Circus* reruns with one dollar and one or two bottles of wine. We would buy twelve or thirteen bottles, drink one, give one to Ben, and then sell the other eleven. So, the thirty-five dollars, or whatever D-Bag and I made between us, was quite a bit of cash for thirteen year olds in 1973, as minimum wage was like a buck sixty, and babysitting jobs paid about a buck an hour.

As for Ben, he became a famous sculptor who provided all of these futuristic, polished, stainless steel pieces for the Austin Powers movies. So, there's a lesson in this tale, but it would take Richard Fucking Feynman or the Maha Fucking Rishi Yogi Berra to figure it out.

JIMMY THE OLD BOXER

People in our neighborhood didn't have a lot of money, but they were happy. All of us had plenty of food and decent shelter and clothing. Sometimes we were a bit short on the extras, though. Between us kids, we usually had enough allowance money to buy a ball to play with, whether it was a twenty-nine-cent Wiffle ball in the summer or a fifty-nine-cent street hockey ball in the winter. A few times, though, we made due with a rock.

But there was a lovely older man, a former boxer, who lived on our street on Bowen Avenue. He was just a sweet, caring person who always offered to help people out with a few bucks or a trip to the grocery store for someone who was laid up. Someone closer to God. Well, one time Jimmy saw us kids playing soccer in the street with a rock.

"Don't you kids gut money for a ball to play with?" asked Jimmy, as he lit one of his ever-present, huge stogies.

"Well, Kenny gets his fifty cent allowance tomorrow, so we can get one then. But this is OK for now," one of us replied.

Jimmy walked on, and we continued to play soccer with our rock. About fifteen minutes later, Jimmy showed up and threw a spongy, white ball into our fray.

"Thanks, Jimmy; you didn't have to do that. I'll pay you back tomorrow," said Kenny.

"It's on me. I just didn't want to see kids in my neighborhood playing ball with a rock. It makes me feel poor."

As usual, Jimmy would deflect someone's thanks and attempt to give a logical reason for why he was such a lovely person. As for me, I don't think someone that kind should be forgotten, someone like Jimmy, the cigar-smoking ex-boxer who lived on Bowen Avenue in Medford, Massachusetts, in the midsixties.

ONE MORE SATURDAY NIGHT, OR ERNEST AND JULIO GALLO ATE MY STOMACH OUT

One more story about Ben. One Saturday night, I was hanging out in D-Bag's kitchen with his long-suffering mom and his unemployed, alky dad. All of a sudden, we heard a car screech its wheels on the busy street in front of the house. Then the car burned rubber and darted for the large kitchen window. Just before the car hit the window, the brakes screeched again, and the car came to a halt. My heart raced as I was sure this was going to be a robbery.

Instead, two burly older guys that I recognized from school opened the two front doors and hauled a third guy from the backseat. The guy was unconscious. When the two big guys had opened the kitchen door and dragged the third guy onto the kitchen floor, we could see that it was Ben. The two big guys fled the kitchen and burned rubber out of the driveway.

We all looked at each other, deadpan. Ben said nothing but writhed on the floor like a beached whale and then slowly barfed. Before any of us could react, Clarkie, the whacked-out pooch, devoured the smelly barf. None of us said anything for a couple of minutes. Finally, Mr. G said, "Well, I guess I'm gonna call it an evening. Goodnight, everyone."

We all did the same.

GOOD THINGS COME IN BLACK AND BLUE PACKAGES

In tenth grade I got into a fight underneath the school bus when it stopped to let kids off. Got my ass kicked, too. The fight happened because one of the school bullies had thrown a snowball and hit a friend of mine in the face. The friend wasn't too angry; I just felt like fighting. And so did the bully.

I called the bitch out, because he had tried to trip me in fourth grade, so I figured I would pay him back with six years' interest. Incorrect. He charged at me unexpectedly and with great speed. Soon he was on top of me punching away. He was punching me very hard. The punches hurt, but more importantly, I was really embarrassed. As the fight moved to underneath the bus, I wound up getting wedged up against the back tire, still trying to fend off a blizzard of punches. Just then, about six of my friends sallied forth from the bus. In seconds, they had beaten the bully down, including lots of kicking when he was down a la Joe Pesci in *Goodfellas.*

One beautiful thing came out of this embarrassing fiasco. Well, two, actually. First of all, my friends proved once again they had my back. I was very grateful for their support and thanked them profusely. I don't see how people can get through life without friends. And that's a no-shitter. Life is too difficult and lonely without pally poohs.

The other groovy thing that came out of my getting my ass kicked under the bus concerned my last friend to get off the bus and help me—Gerry Pascal.

Gerry was a very shy and bookish kid who lived in our neighborhood. To the gang's credit, everyone was nice to him and never hassled him. They did always try to cajole him to play touch football and street hockey, but Gerry would seldom join in.

Gerry used to carry his books tucked into his chest like a girl, and the only reason he got a pass on this was because his sister was pretty popular. Anyway, Gerry unexpectedly walked off the bus behind my friends. He waited until they stopped slapping and punching and kicking the bully, and then he kicked the guy once in the butt and calmly got back on the bus.

And, wouldn't you know it? After that day, Gerry began to lift weights. Then he began to date girls. Then when he graduated high school, he became a state trooper. Now he is a state police captain. I guess it was worth getting beat up if it ended up having such a good effect on someone else's life.

THE MAGIC OF THE SEVENTIES

I went to this party at a nearby town in 1978. The kids at the party all went to the same summer academic program at the local university. At one point at the party, I was sitting in Donna's bedroom, the girl hosting the party. She was sitting on the bed and smoking marijuana with her mother and a few friends. Steely Dan's *Aja* album was playing.

Soon, my friend's twelve-year-old brother barged into the bedroom, announcing, "I just had three hits of THC, and I don't feel a thing."

A few minutes later, he fell unconscious onto the carpeted floor of the bedroom.

Everyone laughed, including his mother, who just took another puff of the marijuana cigarette and mumbled something about her son always acting out.

An attractive, petite, wedge-cut blond woman wearing tight white jeans opened the bedroom door and walked in, accompanied by a strapping eighteen-year-old Nordic-looking guy. They hugged Donna and her mom, and then each took a drag from the joint.

"Who are these guys?" I asked Donna.

"Oh, that's Ms. Parker, and that's Jackie Turner. She's his teacher at our high school. But they're a couple, too."

I must have done a double take, as Donna added, "It's cool, though. They're discreet about it, so no one's gonna get into trouble."

As I took in the scene of my friend's brother still unconscious on the floor, Donna and her mom sharing a joint and laughing on the bed, and the student/ teacher couple cooing on a comfy chair in the corner of the bedroom, I thought, I rather like this excess, or some of it. I'm not sure how much of it I like or what parts of it I like. But I know that this excess won't last. I don't know how I know that, but I know. So, I should just enjoy it while it lasts.

And, of course, Reagan soon showed up. Then the SWAT teams. The Patriot Act and those bitches from social services. But still, in my mind, I sometimes go back to that bedroom and that party and kick back with Steely Dan, loving that moment and knowing in my bones that those times will return.

NOT CHAMPIONSHIP MATERIAL

And there was one other time that I got my ass beat in a high school fight. This time the fight took place in the boy's room. My opponent was Jerry Meade, a short, quiet, slouchy guy who usually minded his own business. I have no idea why we mixed it up in the boy's room of BR High in 1978. Probably just too much testosterone floating around. Or something.

Anyway, I figured I could take this guy. How wrong I was. Although dumpy and slump-shouldered, Jerry was lightning fast, and as soon as you could say, "Mo-foing feces!" he had my head dunked deep in the toilet bowl. I thought I was in big trouble and gonna get whooped. But wouldn't you know it, a couple of my friends grabbed Jerry, slapped him silly, and threw him out.

I thanked my friends, and as they were saying, "Don't mention it," I turned to Jerry and pronounced, "Double life, Walpole."

Number 1: Jerry is doing double life in Walpole as I write this.

Number 2. I don't know why I predicted such a thing. It just came into my head.

Number 3. This prediction started a string of dead-on predictions about friends and acquaintances over the years, and…

Number 4. This was the only time I ever announced a bad prediction. Usually, if I see something bad that's going to happen in someone's life, I'll just shut up about it, or I will try to give a touch of gentle advice to steer that person in the right direction. That's assuming that I know what the right direction is.

As far as predictions go, I have made four major ones concerning the lives of my friends. They have all been dead on.

1. Caroline. Ten years before Caroline ever picked up a musical instrument, I predicted that she would be a rock star. She just gave me the middle finger and said that I was crazy. Ten years later, she got this Asian-American boyfriend who was a hot guitarist. He soon taught her to play pretty good bass guitar. Then they formed a band. They moved to Buffalo and went unnoticed. They moved to LA and were extra-unnoticed. Then they moved to San Francisco and began playing coffee houses. Their sound was sort of a funky, pop, bluesy thing. At a San Francisco performance, this French tourist buys a five-dollar CD from the band. A month later, Caroline gets a call from Sony France to come to Paris and cut a CD. Twenty-nine gold records later, and Caroline is a rock star all over Europe.

2. Jazz. My friend Jazz worked at Qualcomm phone company just as its stock was about to go into orbit in 1999. She had a lot of stock options that would vest in a couple of years. However, Jazz went part time for a year so she could go to massage school. A month later, Qualcomm laid off all part-timers. A month after that, Qualcomm stock went into orbit, making those stock options worth a fortune. So, adios Jazz, and adios stock options. I consoled Jazz by predicting that she would also become a millionaire within five years. She opened the door to her room, where she was crying, and gave me the finger and threw her furry George Bush slipper at me. She then told me that people don't live their lives to fulfill my fantasies. But they do. After six months, many of our friends at Qualcomm became millionaires, as Qualcomm stock climbed from forty-five dollars a share to seven hundred and forty dollars per share. For a time, Jazz cursed me even more, but I held firm with my prediction. Don't defy the oracle. Anyway, a few months later, Jazz moved to California to work at Google. Four years later, she retired as a multimillionaire from her Google options and moved to London.

3. Mr. Sammo. Mr. Sammo and I were buds from fourth grade to twelfth grade. One time in Miss Martin's sixth-grade reading class, I casually told Mr. Sammo that he would be a vice-president of a major corporation by the time he was forty. He asked me why I said that, and I told him that I just smelled the aroma of that future. Mr. Sammo became a vice-president of a major corporation at thirty-eight years of age.

4. Mitt is Australian. He moved to the United States with his family. His dad is an investment banker here in the States. Both Mitt and his dad dislike the monarchy in Australia and wish for a republican government there. However, I predicted that Mitt would one day possess a noble title. Mitt also hates the nobility and just gave me the middle finger and told me to fuck off when I told him my prediction. Many years later, Mitt's dad buys a chateau in southwestern France so his family members still in Australia might be enticed to visit him more often, as the flight from Australia to the United States is a bitch. And, what do you know? Dip me in dog poo if that European chateau didn't include the noble title of baron. Don't defy the oracle, kids.

5. My neighborhood friend, Ron. For some reason, I looked at Ron one day as we were playing touch football with a bunch of other kids from the neighborhood, and I said to myself that one day Ron would do time in prison for pedophilia. I have no idea what made me think this. I take no pleasure that this prophecy was also correct.

AND I THOUGHT MY FAMILY WAS FUCKED-UP

Many years later, I was a guest at D-Bag's house for Thanksgiving. Before any food was served, everyone in D-Bag's family started fighting with each other.

"You're not getting drunk this holiday!" screeched Mrs. G at Mr. G as he took his seat at the table.

"Just one little drink, Mommy," said Mr. G.

"The turkey isn't gonna be dry again this time, is it, Mom? added D-Bag at just the wrong moment.

Mrs. G slammed the cooked turkey on the table and ran upstairs to her bedroom. Mr. G followed a moment later. Screaming and arguing was heard from upstairs.

D-Bag, Ben, and I looked at each other for a few minutes. Then Ben went upstairs to his room. D-Bag looked at me for a few minutes and left the house. I sat dumbfounded for a few minutes. I didn't leave, though, as I thought everyone would recover and return momentarily. A few minutes later, Mrs. G returned to the table, only to put the turkey in the fridge. She then hurried upstairs without a word. Fortunately, McDonald's was open, so I had a quarter pounder with cheese for ninety-one cents, including tax.

And I thought my family was fucked up.

THE AGE OF GUNPOWDER

I blew up my seventeenth birthday cake. It was a white cake with chocolate frosting that a friend, Lady Jane, brought over. Don't know why I did it. I must have been overcome by exuberance. Or maybe I was laughing at the idea of counting one's age. Anyway, just as Lady Jane was putting wax candles on the cake, something came over me, and I ran into my room and found a pack of firecrackers. I seeded the cake with the ordinance and fired the crackers up. I then grabbed the cake and bolted outside. Everyone was shocked (but amused) and followed me out, shouting with glee. I just made it to the hood of my butterscotch orange 1969 Ford LTD when the top blew off the cake.

Then we ate the cake. It tasted a bit gun powdery, but it had a nice chocolate flavor.

HOLY GESTAPO, BATMAN!

And another thing; a couple of my friends' dads were in the Gestapo.

I had one friend in high school, Dierk, and we used to play war games at his house. Many times, his dad, Ulli, would stop in to say hello. Ulli had an import-export business and was also interested in antiquities. I also loved antiquities and enjoyed those times when Ulli would show me stuff, like a cool Athenian owl cup from the fifth century BC or a small Corinthian terracotta statue of Aphrodite from the same period. Sometimes Dierk would show me cool stuff from his collection, too, like silver Alexander the Great coins from the fourth century BC.

One time, Dierk asked me if I wanted to see his dad's old army uniform. I said OK, not expecting to see anything very interesting, just maybe a US Army sergeant's uniform. Instead, when Dierk came out of his dad's bedroom and shook the garment seductively on its hanger, it turned out to be a lieutenant's uniform from the Gestapo.

"Well, dip me in poo," I exclaimed with more surprise than I let on.

Dierk smiled impishly and added, "Exactly."

Ulli was a really sweet guy, but how he got into the United States after being in the Gestapo was a mystery wrapped up in a conundrum and tied into a neat gordian knot and placed in a Neiman Marcus shopping bag.

When I worked in the kitchen at the University of Colorado, one of my co-workers was this crazed German-American lady named Susan. Susan was always singing country music and taking off on the weekends to meet cowboys, to the consternation of her ever-loving husband, Stan.

One time, as the rest of the staff were having their lunch break in the dining room, along with about one hundred students, Susan sailed into the dining room and showed us all a photograph of her father.

"Gee, Dad looked so handsome in his Gestapo uniform. It's a shame I can't display it in my bedroom. My husband said he wouldn't sleep there if I did."

"Why don't you hang it in your living room?" I asked, trying to appear nonchalant.

"I tried that, but my friends said they wouldn't come over until I took the picture down."

"Your dad does look great in that picture, Susan. Maybe you should keep it on the backside of the door to one of your closets," I added, trying to be helpful.

Susan's dad really seemed like a nice guy to me.

File the whole affair under *W* for WTF.

YOU NOT SO DIRTY RAT

My dad was a plumber in the navy and then went to HVAC school to learn how to be a refrigeration and air conditioning maintenance guy. Dad worked for a big company during the week, but during the weekends, he did side jobs with his drunken navy buddies. Dad took side plumbing and air conditioning jobs on the weekends to help out his navy friends, who often found themselves unemployed after getting fired for drunkenness.

On many jobs there was a task that consisted of going down into some dark and smelly space to turn on or turn off a water valve or some such thing. That's where I came in.

Dad would hand me two wrenches.

"The small wrench is to shut off the main water valve. Turn it counterclockwise, like I told you. The bigger wrench is for rats. If a rat looks hostile, hit him over the head before he bites you."

I did see a rat once. One of Dad's buddies lowered me down into a hole in the side of a wall at some run-down school in Boston. After a few seconds, this sweet-looking big guy rat came up to me, almost as if to be petted. And I was almost tempted to pet him, but he veered off at the last second.

And I made five dollars a day for these maneuvers. Good money when the minimum wage was a dollar forty an hour.

IT'S A BOY! AND IT'S ME.

I remember being born. That memory came back to me over a videotape-watching session during freshman football. I shouldn't have been playing freshman football, I should have been starring at another high school as a soccer goalkeeper, but I'm a frigging idiot. And I'll tell that story a bit later.

Anyway, I remember being born because of the school bully, Pudge. Well, actually, Pudge is a very nice person, but a bully, too. Anyway, as we members of the freshman football team sat in a dark room watching dark, out of focus videos of our last game, Pudge snuck up behind us and squeezed our stomachs with both hands as hard as he could. And Pudge was a big, strong guy.

I was having a really difficult time following the game on the video. The videographer, Jonathon Preen, was terrible. He didn't know anything about football. He set up his camera at one end of the field and never moved it. Sometimes the wind would swivel his camera away from the action, and it would take Jonathon five minutes to sort it out, as he was watching the girls in the crowd and not the game through his camera.

And Jonathon was nuts anyway. Carmine had told me for years that Jonathon had bottled his own semen in Coke bottles and stored them in the rafters of the garage of his mom's house where he still lived at the age of thirty. I never believed that story until Carmine and I, drunk on Mateus wine supplied by his brother, Bones, barged into Jonathon's mother's unlocked garage. Once there, Carmine found a step stool and began handing me these dusty old Coke bottles with about an inch of some dried, greenish-white substance that appeared to be jizz.

File it under *O* for "Oy-vay." Or *J* for Jesus H. Christ.

Anyway, when Pudge got around to squeezing my stomach as hard as he could, I made an effort to be nonchalant about it. Everyone else had cried out, "Cut it out, Pudge. That fuckin' hurts."

So, Pudge conceded that I was a pretty tough dude. Not as tough as Pudge, though. He could definitely kick my ass. One time I arm-wrestled him, and it was like trying to move a brick wall; he was that strong.

Anyway, I woke up at about two that morning, and this memory came to me. Prompted by Pudge's shenanigans, I believe; I remembered being born.

I remembered this terrible feeling of tightness. Much like the tightness I felt that afternoon when Pudge had squeezed my stomach really hard. Then I remember being stuck in a very tight space for a really long time. Then I remember feeling really scared and being held upside down by the doctor. I was freaking out, screaming.

Then the doctor slapped my ass really hard. I felt hate for the doctor. And I remember thinking that I didn't want to be there and wanted to quickly go back to where I came from—either the womb or nonexistence. Then I remember my mom saying to me as I howled, "That's OK; he's supposed to do that. He has to hit your bottom to see if you're breathing."

My mom didn't believe that I remembered being born. She said that I was full of shit.

Until I told her the exact words that I just wrote to you guys.

THE WORLD OF SAMMY'S WONG

On a lighter note, my friend, Sammy, dated this adorable Jewish girl named Debbie in eighth grade. I was crazy about Debbie and asked her out in both fifth and seventh grade, but it was "no go" for me. We were pals, though.

Sammy also had an enormous schlong. How do I know? Sammy was in my gym class, and we took showers together after dodgeball or crab soccer or all the other stupid games we had to play in gym class. Therefore I was in a position to know, and so did the whole town, because it had like eleven thousand people in it, for Christ's sake.

Anyway, in February of eighth grade, I was throwing a winter party and sent out invitations to my thirty closest friends. The invitation cards happened to have a cartoon drawing of a rhino on them. So, of course, I had to elongate the rhino's horn with a pen and add the caption, "Sammy's Wong," alongside of it.

A few days later, my mom got a bunch of phone calls from some of my friends' moms.

Some of my female friends' moms, that is. Several of the moms admitted that the invitation was funny but that it was too adult for the eighth-grade crowd. So, I had to apologize to the moms and promise to never do such a thing again. What else could I do? The reality was that such a gag not only wasn't too adult for the eighth-grade crowd, but it was too juvenile to them. That's why I made the gag. It was just trite and silly and not daring at all.

I could never follow Mr. Sinatra's advice to young comedians: "Kid, don't work blue."

Fortunately, it was the seventies, so none of the moms contacted the school principal, the school psychologist, (who would have just cracked up, anyway), the SWAT teams, the purveyors of Adderall and Ritalin, or...that bitch from social services.

The upstart of all this silliness is that Debbie's dad, Aaron, saw the invitation and banned me from his house. He especially banned me from attending Debbie's bat mitzvah. I crashed the party anyway, since Aaron was always at the office, and Debbie's mom was really cool.

There was a bit of payback from Debbie's mom, though. Mrs. H snuck up behind me as I was gabbing away at the buffet table and stuffed an enormous portion of liverwurst on matzo cracker into my gob. Then she pressed her hand against my mouth to prevent my spitting out the offending foodstuff.

"It's good, isn't it?"

I thought, it's actually not bad, but not my favorite. The liverwurst almost grew on me, but not quite. It wasn't terrible, but I knew that I would never eat liverwurst again.

Ironically, or not, I have been a victim of having funky foods snuck into my gob by several Jewish moms at several Jewish parties. Why me? I really love Jewish people. I think they are amazing. They have been forced to do the crappy jobs for centuries. Then they do a brilliant job at all those occupations, like surgeons and bankers, and some people are jealous that they are so fucking talented. I can't believe that there are only twenty million Jews in the world. You would think that there are four billion of them, because they punch so much above their weight.

Anyway, my aunt worked at a large Ford dealership that was owned by two Jewish brothers. The two bosses were just lovely, as were their wives. My aunt rose all the way from the secretarial pool to president of the company. At Barry and his wife's twenty-fifth anniversary party (my aunt's bosses were always sweet enough to invite us to many parties, too), I was gibbering away like a rhesus monkey at the buffet table when this hand reached around from behind me and crammed a cracker with creamed herring into my big mouth.

"Isn't that good?" asked Mrs. R, with the genuine hope in her eye that I would agree.

"It's a little funky and smoky and fishy," I said, but it was something that I could eat once in a while.

At another party, Mrs. R struck again, this time cramming a piece of bread loaded with fish eggs into my chute.

"Whattaya think of that?"

I thought it tasted pretty salty and funky. But, ten years later, I reflected upon that experience and decided that I liked caviar. But I can only afford the cheapo American varieties like flying fish roe and not the beluga that was prominent at Barry's dos.

PAPA MADE A BRAND NEW HOLE

My dad would get pretty angry often. Ragey, crazy, break-shit angry. One time Dad came home drunk while I was watching James Brown on TV. James Brown was dancing around like crazy. There were also two attendants on stage constantly wiping James Brown's forehead with a cloth or changing his scarves. I think it was those two guys that set Dad off. He looked at the performance on television for a few minutes in utter amazement. Then he flew into a rage, picked up a chair, and was just about to throw it into the TV when my mom grabbed his arm.

"Don't break my TV. It's too expensive to replace."

"I can't stand that goddamn uppity nigger."

"He's really good, though," said my mom, thoughtfully.

Another time, my dad came home really pissed off, because he had wanted his company to hire a friend of his, one of his drunken navy buds, but Dad's boss told him that he had to hire a minority, instead.

"Jimmy is more fuckin' qualified than that fuckin' coon!" screamed Dad as he picked up a kitchen chair and slammed it into the wall, making a huge hole in the drywall. Again he slammed the chair into the wall, making a bigger hole. I was scared shitless. I thought he was going to come after my mom or me. In fact, I always thought Dad would kill us all. He would get so angry. Fortunately, this time he just jumped into his car and peeled out of the driveway like fucking crazy.

Dad ended up killing my step mom, though, but that was many years later. And I wasn't present at those festivities.

I FORGOT THE FIVE

One day, my dad got the notion that I should learn the concept of numbers one through ten. He also thought I should learn how to add and subtract the numbers one through ten. This episode took place about a year before I started kindergarten. So, I must have been five years old.

Dad would take a deck of cards and deal two cards facedown. Say a two and a six. He would then ask rapid fire, "What's two and six?"

I didn't quite get the idea of addition. I would guess a number, which was usually wrong. Dad would then fly into a range at the idea that I didn't understand addition and angrily slapped me across the face with a lot of force.

"What's six minus two!?" Dad would bark. I was whimpering helplessly.

"What's six minus two!?"

"Seven?" I would guess, shivering in fear. Dad would slap me across the face even harder. My mother would try to intervene.

"Shut up!" Dad would bark at Mom. Then he would draw two more cards.

"Five and four. What's five minus four!?"

I couldn't think, because I felt so helpless and alone. My mom tried to whisper the answer to me, and she got slapped across the face for her troubles.

"I ain't raising no fucking imbeciles!" snarled Dad as he dealt two more cards. I have never felt so helpless and friendless. Usually these sessions would last twenty or thirty minutes, and afterward, Dad would still be so fucking pissed off that he would get into his car and burn rubber down the street to the pub. Life seldom gets this scary, kids. Mostly downhill from here.

THE BROTHERHOOD OF THE PORN

I had a really good friend in high school by the name of Carmine Pallone, or Tito to his friends. Tito was short and skinny, with long, stringy blonde hair. I met Tito under curious circumstances. A schoolmate, Aaron Pincus, had a dad who was a college professor. His dad was also into skin magazines. Mostly *Playboy*, *Penthouse*, *Cavalier*, *Screw*, and *Hustler*. And *Knave* and *Oui* and *Puritan*. Aaron's dad used to let Aaron read his skin magazines in the garage at their house where the magazines were kept. Soon enough, Aaron invited many of his school chums to check out the skin mags and get some education. I met Tito one day as we were both admiring the centerfold models of our respective magazines, and we both happened to show the other the centerfold we were admiring. We were fast friends. This phenomenon happens in Tokyo a lot. If you're in a shop that sells stroke material, you often see two Japanese guys sharing the sight of their respective skin mags and then becoming fast friends.

I grew to know and admire the Pallone family. They were a lovely bunch of people. His mom was a gracious, loving woman who had many talents and good sense. She would often play lovely classical pieces on the piano, and it was Mrs. Pallone who had the sense to sell the family's Yahoo stock before it crashed, preserving a huge capital gain.

"It's time to sell. I can feel it in my bones. It's starting to feel like the great stock bubble in the twenties. I was just a little girl then, but I remember the atmosphere."

Mr. Pallone was the school athletic director. He was a little fireball. Always chairing sports committees, refereeing matches, or just flitting around the house making repairs. Mr. Pallone was a sweet and caring person, and he was so good to me. He also knew a great many sports celebrities. Mr. P had been a great college second baseman at Boston College and played many games against excellent Negro League teams. In one game, Mr. Pallone went two for three against the great pitcher, William Jackman. Mr. P also held the college record for most plate appearances without making an out. In fact, Mr. P was drafted by the Brooklyn Dodgers to compete with Jackie Robinson for the starting job at second base. Mr. P had a family by that time and decided to remain as a coach and athletic director in Massachusetts instead of playing baseball.

Whenever I went to the Pallones', I never knew who might show up. But whenever they had someone special over for dinner, Mr. P always asked me to join the party. One time Larry Doby showed up for dinner; he was a great baseball player for the Cleveland Indians.

Larry was the first black ballplayer to play in the American League. He was also a sweetie. Larry told me that he thought it might have been easier to be a baseball player before the days of airline travel. He thought the shorter distances between teams allowed the players to travel the four hundred to eight hundred miles by train in a more relaxing fashion. Larry said that the players would play cards into the night and crash in sleeping cars. He said that with air travel, baseball could spread to more faraway cities. This caused the players to cross more time zones and constantly suffer jet lag.

ENTERTAINING MR. WILLIAMS

One time I went over to the Pallones' in the afternoon and sat in the kitchen, waiting for Carmine to come down from upstairs, where he was finishing up some homework. Mr. P had his head under the faucet in the kitchen, dyeing his hair. Mr. P, who was fifty-eight at the time, said he would dye his hair until he was sixty, because he was still getting job offers and didn't want to look like an old fart if he decided to show up for an interview. "After sixty, I'll go gray," promised Mr. P. And that's what he did when he turned sixty. I feel the same way. I'm fifty-two now, and I dye my hair with rosemary tea that I keep cool in a bottle. I use about a half teaspoon in my hair every couple of days and keep it on for an hour. Then I shower and shampoo my hair.

Anyway, after listening to Mr. P discuss his philosophy of hair dyeing for men, the phone rang. Mr. P grabbed the phone, which had a one hundred-foot cord. He talked for a few minutes and then handed the receiver to me.

"Tell Ted to stop being a jerk and come to dinner tonight," instructed Mr. P.

"Who's Ted?" I asked.

"Ted Williams. He gets shy sometimes. You have dinner with us, too. But don't talk baseball, and don't ask for autographs."

I would never ask for autographs. Unless Elizabeth Hurley showed up. Or Gordon Banks. Or Nobby Stiles. Or Hayley Mills.

"Hi, Mr. Williams. Mr. Pallone said don't be a jerk, and come to dinner tonight."

"He said what? Tell Larry that I just don't feel like meeting new people today. He said you're a really good guy, though."

"Uh-huh. Why don't you come to dinner tonight, and I'll stay home. I don't want to mess up your evening."

"No, don't be a jerk. I'm sorry; I'm being the jerk. I just get funny sometimes, you know? I don't feel like meeting new people just now. You go to dinner, and tell Larry I'll call him later in the week."

"Will you tell Ted to quit being a jerk and come to dinner tonight. Margie made lasagna just like he likes it, and Karen made the chocolate chip cookies," pleaded Mr. P. One time during the Vietnam War, Carmine's sister, Karen, had made six dozen of her delicious chocolate chip cookies to send to her cousin in Vietnam, as she did every month. Mr. Williams happened to come over that day and started eating the cookies. Well, those cookies were so good that Mr. Williams ended up eating all six dozen of them, because he just couldn't stop. He apologized profusely to Karen, who is a loving sweetheart. Karen just laughed and said that she was glad Ted liked the cookies. Karen then made seven dozen more. One dozen for Mr. Williams and another six dozen for her cousin.

"I heard that. Tell Larry to quit being a jerk, and I'll call him Friday."

"Mr. P, Mr. Williams said for you to quit being a jerk, and he'll call you back later."

I bet a million kids dreamed of meeting Mr. Williams, but when I get to meet him, it was over the phone in the middle of an argument about dinner. And I never got to have dinner with Mr. Williams, but there were other celebs to hang with over at the Pallones'.

Carmine's cousin was Steve Balboni, the great slugger for the Yankees and Royals. Steve visited the Pallones' in Bridgewater quite often. Steve was a warm, witty, intelligent Italian-American kid who liked to play Wiffleball. We had a lot of fun playing in the Pallones' backyard. I managed to get Steve out a few times with my sidearm curve that goes up and down and up. Steve said that if I could throw that pitch in the majors, I could have a good career.

At the risk of becoming annoying, I will relate another of my celebrity sightings at the Pallones'. What am I saying? I am annoying. And that's not going to change. Also, what do people like reading about today except celebrity crap, tales of madness, silliness, grossness, and sex? Well, it's all here, folks.

HOLY HEMORRHOIDS, UNCLE CHARLIE!

Anyway, another time that I was at the Pallones', listening to Earth, Wind, and Fire records with Carmine and reading his brothers old *Playboy* magazines, Mrs. P came into Carmine's room downstairs, totally cool about the *Playboy* magazines, by the way, and informed Carmine that we'd hung around the house so late in the afternoon that we had to help serve the brunch at her garden club get-together. That sounded pretty boring to us. Until William Demarest showed up. William Demarest played Uncle Charley on *My Three Sons*, a favorite show of mine in the late sixties.

I asked Mr. Demarest what he was doing at Mrs. Pallone's garden club party of all places.

"What am I doing here? I'm a member. That's what I'm doing here. Margie and I go way back. She used to be a showgirl in the thirties. That was when I was breaking into the pictures. We used to be an item."

I told Mr. Demarest that I really respected the wisdom of older people and asked him what life advice he could give to a fifteen-year-old person like myself.

"Always eat your fiber. Make sure you can take a good shit every day. I got these fucking hemorrhoids, because I never ate right. And I still don't. Eat your oatmeal and your vegetables, OK, Kid?"

I never forgot that advice. It did take me a few years to let the advice sink in. But after a few episodes of constipation and a sore *culo*, I remembered Mr.

Demarest's advice and started eating my vegetables. I also like to drink a shake containing spinach and apple juice every day. I figured that if it worked for Popeye, it would work for me. See, the simplest observations are often the best.

FOOD FIGHT I

As for food fights, I've experienced two. One night in junior year of high school, D-Bag called and said to meet the gang at the Papa Gino's in Raynham. I replied that I didn't have the cash on me for pizza. I had money in the bank, but there were no ATM machines in those days. D-Bag told me to just show up, and someone would lend me seventy-five cents for a slice of pizza.

But when I got to Papa Gino's, the joint was stinky with our archenemies, the kids from neighboring Middleboro. There was a shouting match going on between the Middleboro contingent on one side of the restaurant and our guys on the other side. Remember that our guys had gotten into a big rumble with the Middleboro guys in the past, and our guys beat the crap out of the those bums with baseball bats. So, it looked like the rival host was after revenge.

Since I didn't see any baseball bats, and since going back home seemed like a depressing prospect, I walked over to my friends and said hello. I ignored the abuse and threats that were hurled my way.

"What a fuckin' pussy!" one guy yelled.

"I'm gonna kick your fuckin' ass!" came another threat from a rather large and strong-looking guy with big bushy hair and eyebrows.

Just as I wondered whether to say or do anything in response to this unsolicited abuse, I saw slices of pizza start to fly in both directions across the restaurant. Since I was hungry, I intercepted a slice flying by and ate it quickly. I then seized a second slice and downed it quickly, too. It tasted delicious. And it was free. A third slice (pepperoni) sailed face down onto a friend's lime green parka, which was sitting on a table nearby. I snatched the slice off the jacket and ate it. I'll never forget the huge grease stain that the slice had imprinted on the jacket, like a crime scene outline of a dead body in pepperoni juice.

"Gross!" and "Disgusting!" were the shouts of disapproval from both sides of the room when they saw me grab the pizza slice off the coat. I received more vilification by grabbing another slice that sat facedown on the carpeted floor of the dining room. Damn, that tasted good. Who said there was no such thing as a free lunch?

As I was munching the fourth slice of Papa Gino's, someone put their arm around my neck in a friendly manner. It was the big guy with the bushy hair who had just threatened to kick my fucking ass two minutes ago. He looked at me with the regard of a genuine fellow feeling.

"You don't have to eat pizza off the floor, man. Let me buy you a slice and a Coke."

"That's very nice of you, but I'm reveling in the warpage of this silly scene," I responded, quite touched by this guy's generosity, especially since this was the guy who had threatened to beat my fuckin' ass.

"Look at this silliness. Isn't it great?" I exuded, pointing to the slices and Cokes flying through the air. The big guy took in the scene and laughed with a twinkle in his eye. I then picked a piece of pizza off the carpet and handed it to the big guy.

"Enjoy."

I laughed. The big guy let a big roar and munched the slice with gusto. We both just laughed and shook our heads in mutual relish of the moment. That's life for you. One minute a guy wants to slap you silly, and the next minute he wants to buy you dinner. No need to figure it out; it was the seventies, man.

FOOD FIGHT II

The one other food fight I've been involved with took place the Wednesday afternoon before Thanksgiving break in eighth grade. The food fight started just a moment after Mr. Feely, the vice principal, had wished us a nice four-day Thanksgiving vacation over the intercom. Immediately after, Patsy O'Connor let loose with a plastic sporkful of mashed potato. The reconstituted mashed potatoes and chicken gravy landed on Pudge's purple polka dotted polyester shirt. Pudge stared down the entire crowd of kids for several seconds and then bolted upright from his chair with surprising speed. Pudge let out a roar and seized every bit of food on his tray and that of his dining companions, lobbing a disgusting fusillade of funky seventies chow in every possible direction.

The damage caused by Pudge was very democratic in nature. D-Bag took some greasy green bean casserole thingy to his new practice drum pad. Tito received a salvo of buttery corn on his new white jeans. This offering of food prompted the normally mild mannered Tito to load up his spork with braised beef in gravy and hurl it into the fray, accompanied by frenzied screaming. Tito kept loading up his spork and launching the contents at the enemy until his lunch tray was completely empty. One of his last broadsides scored a direct hit on the lime green suede flares of Mrs. Gruman's (the lunch monitor) mod pantsuit. Before she could get a word in, Mr. Feely started to bellow over the intercom. "This is an outrage! Stop this instant. I have never experienced such lawlessness and savagery in my thirteen years as principal of this school. You should all be ashamed of yourselves! I will be down in five minutes. If this madness has not stopped, I will call the police, and there will be arrests!"

This tirade only intensified the amount of green bean casserole thingy, braised beef thingy, spice cake, dinner rolls, Jell-O, milk, and water that flew through the air. This expended food ammo was beginning to form quite a crust on the surface of the dining room carpet. This crust was becoming so high that I couldn't see much of the carpet's former puke-green color anymore. And a lot of kids were wearing serious amounts of chow. Tito had received a load of Jell-O on his checked farmer's shirt. Danny Mooney was sitting in shock. He had just taken a milk bath. His clothes were soaked, and there was about a pint of milk in a puddle dripping from the tabletop down to his lap. I had something in my hair resembling fake whipped cream. I looked like an extra in a Ron Jeremy film.

To add to the Chaplinesqueness of this scene, Mr. Feely ran into the dining room with a bullhorn, promptly slipped on the government-issue grub crust on the carpet, and took a header into the ooze. Cue madcap laughter and vigorous clapping.

Pure seventies mayhem and excess at its finest!

"I will call the police in three minutes if this circus does not desist!" warned Mr. Feely, as he gingerly walked through the muck and consulted Mrs. Gruman, whose huge blond wig was starting to attract a lot of milk and Jell-O. After a brief chat, Mr. Feely grabbed Pudge and his sidekick, Sly, by the ears and double-timed them out of the lunchroom.

Fortunately or unfortunately, the Great Williams Middle School Food Fight of 1974 came to an end, but only because we ran out of food. It didn't end with a whimper but with a long and loud lecture from Mr. Feely over the intercom. The highlight was the following confession: "As many of you know, I was in psychotherapy for many decades. I have felt well for many years." Mr. Feely then began to break down, openly weeping. "But now I will be returning to therapy. Damn you, you little bastards!"

Huge laughter and clapping. A standing ovation followed for a couple of minutes. I hid under the table. I didn't know what else to do. Don't kick a man when he's down, you know?

When we came back from Thanksgiving vacation the following Monday, the pile of food on the floor had turned to a tall, thick crust of grunge. We spent about an hour at lunch shoveling the food from the carpet into large trash barrels lined with Hefty bag liners.

We were lectured by Mr. Feely over the intercom through the entire cleanup.

"Clean. Clean. Work. You beasts. Uncivilized animals. Anyone caught laughing will be given detention."

Really, this should have been a scene from a Fellini film, with this soliloquy given by a priest who was really a chick in drag. The only way I could keep from cracking up with geysers of wild cackling was to concentrate on the sight of Mrs. Gruman's new fake zebra print boots in shiny polyurethane. I was trying to imagine rodgering Mrs. Gruman from the backside with her up against the wall as her boots slipped and slid into the ooze of the violated carpet in the lunchroom.

And if that isn't sick enough, Mrs. Gruman was also my mom's pal. But the thing about Mrs. Gruman was that she was like a Barbie doll, with so many neat wigs and outfits and shoes. I love that shit. I fucking hate hippie chicks.

That's Earl, brother.

PS: The field trip to the artsy fartsy crafts workshop got cancelled to pay for cleaning the lunchroom carpet. A good thing, too. Fuck those hippie posers.

DAD'S GRASSY KNOLL

One early morning when I woke up to watch the *Major Mudd Show* on Boston television, I couldn't find the show. The spaceship-motif cartoon show was on channel seven. Even though the channel seven logo was imprinted on a TV show that was playing at that moment, the *Major Mudd Show* was not playing. On channel seven was some live news thing. I saw a casket on an old-fashioned wagon. A horse was pulling the wagon. I didn't know what was going on with channel seven. I loved the *Major Mudd Show*, because the host played this astronaut on a spaceship whose equipment was always acting screwy. Sometimes the doors would fail to open on Major Mudd's arm commands. And many times the ship's robot would get mad at Major Mudd and step on his foot. Plus, Major Mudd often played the Three Stooges, whose slapstick comedy I love.

As I was trying to figure out why this boring wagon show was on TV instead of Major Mudd, my dad walked out of his bedroom on the way to the bathroom to get ready for work.

"What's this show about, Dad? Where's Major Mudd?"

"Your Major Mudd show isn't on today, because they killed that bastard. Kennedy was a communist piece of shit, and that's why they killed him. He got what he deserved."

Dad marched into the bathroom and slammed the door. Evidently, Dad wasn't buying the lone-gunman theory from the get-go.

DON'T EVER BECOME A COP!

One of my aunt's brothers was on a big city police department for thirty years. One time I asked him if he liked being a police officer. He said that he really didn't, and if I ever became a cop, he would beat my ass. Uncle Billy said he joined the force to help people, but he soon found out that the police force was a shit show. At the end of the first week, he was given a brown paper bag that contained a lot of cash.

"What's this for?" asked Uncle Billy of his sergeant.

"That's this week's bonus."

"What's the bonus for?"

"It's your share of the tips we got this week."

"Why do we get tips?"

"For the good service that we do. Some people give us tips." The sergeant looked at Billy like he was an idiot. Billy's face finally emitted a show of comprehension as to what these tips might be for.

"What if I don't want to take this week's tips?" asked Billy.

The sergeant's face got very red, and he yelled, "If you don't take the bonus this week and every week, the bonus that you deserve, you will have no friends on this department. No one will back you up in a shootout. No one will back you up if you have any problems with internal affairs, if you have any problems with a citizen. You will be persona non grata. So, take the bonus."

Billy took the bonus, but he had problems with taking the bonus. Billy had so many problems with taking the bonus that periodically he would check himself into a mental institution. Every time he came out, though, he would go back to the police force until he had thirty years in, and then he retired.

TAKE IT FROM A PRO:

One time, when I was a junior in high school, I got home at about one in the morning from a drunken evening of watching our school hockey team get beaten down by a neighboring school. Our team was pretty good, but all of the other teams in the league were better. I think I drank a half pint of vodka and a bottle of Boone's Farm strawberry wine. I remember taunting a friend at the penalty box who had gotten into a fight during the game. I blacked out at that point, and the next thing I remembered was puking violently on the lawn in the back of our house. As I puked, I noticed someone put their head really close to mine. The person smelled like whisky. It was my dad.

"I've spent my life doing what you're doing right now, and I don't recommend it."

Dad then disappeared into the house. I felt awful for days. So awful that I only got sick one more time from booze. That last time that I got sick on booze was the time I went out to Cape Cod for broiled lobster with Arch Carpenter. As we were driving back, I opened up the door to Arch's sporty Firebird and barfed on the road for about a minute.

I never saw Arch again, as we both went in separate directions to our respective colleges. About ten years later, I was told a story about Arch. He was traveling back from a boozy day on Cape Cod. Someone else was driving. Once back in Bridgewater, Arch opened the passenger door and began throwing up. Just at that moment, the driver of the car was so drunk that he didn't know he was driving on the sidewalk and managed to drive Arch's head into a telephone pole. Arch was killed instantly.

JUST A TYPICAL EVENING

A typical evening at our house would begin with my mom periodically emerging from her bedroom in a valium and TV haze. She would knock on my bedroom door, and I would be sitting on my bed also using the TV as a narcotic.

"Where's your goddamn father?" she would begin, reciting the script.

"I dunno," I would say in a depressed daze.

My mother would look at me with disgust and moan, "He's out drinking again with his goddamned floozies."

"I dunno."

"I can't take this anymore!" my mother would scream.

"OK," I would reply.

"Oh, you're no use," my mom would say as she walked back to her bedroom and slammed the door.

I would spend the next several hours doing homework, feeling depressed, and watching TV. *Charlie's Angels, Three's Company, Laverne & Shirley.* Sometimes I would call up friends to see if they wanted to go to McDonald's or just talk. Anything to feel better.

I would make sure to be in bed and turn the lights out before midnight, because that's when my dad would usually stagger home.

The very second my dad opened the door, my mom would start in on him.

"Out drinking again. You drunk!"

"I like my friends."

"You're an alcoholic!"

"I'm a drunk. Not an alcoholic."

"You're pathetic."

"I'm Happy." At this point, Dad would usually go on the offensive. "What's for supper?"

"I have some cold spaghetti and sauce. I have to warm it up. Supper was at five o'clock, remember?"

Then Dad, on cue, would sound murderous. "I want meat!"

Mom would become scared. "All the m-m-meat is in the freezer. I have to thaw it out."

Then Dad would slap Mom and maybe throw a chair.

"I have to thaw it out," Mom would say helplessly.

"I want it now! Now!"

Then my mother would squeal in pain. Probably Dad had twisted her arm behind her back.

"OK, OK. Stop. I'll make it as soon as I can."

"Now!"

I always tried to shut down my emotions as completely as possible. I never even considered attempting to intervene on my mom's behalf; it just would have made things worse. I would have been beaten down and probably thrown out of the house. Besides, I couldn't cut it on my own on the outside. It was up to my mom to leave the man. Otherwise, we would continue having these scenes two to six times per week as we had for many years. As for me, I quickly learned to become numb to it. But the problem with being numb to it was that it was very hard to get un-numb when I wanted to. You can't just turn it on and off.

COULD'A GONE PRO

I started to play soccer because of Stiv Lundquist. We were sitting in Mr. Potemkin's class during a lull in the action. Mr. P had popped out to his locker to get these replica Greek vases from his recent trip to Athens. Just as Mr. P popped out of the room, someone started poking me in the back with a finger.

"How come you're such a pathetic puss?" came the truculent inquiry from Stiv, a skinny red-haired Swedish-American. Stiv was a mellow, sweet guy when he wasn't on his high horse and all stirred up.

"I don't know."

"You said you would come out for basketball last year, and you never showed."

"Huh?"

"We need a goalie for our soccer team. Show up Saturday morning at eleven at Legion Field."

"What?"

"You have plenty of time to beat your meat and still play soccer."

"Beat my what? I don't know how to play soccer."

"You don't have to know how to play fucking soccer. You just have to keep the goddamn ball out of the fucking net."

Stiv was really worked up. So, I showed up, and the coach put me in goal at Stiv's insistence. And I played well. Evidently I developed a good deal of agility playing the makeshift ball games that poor city kids played in their cramped circumstances. Stickball. Wiffleball. Street hockey. Punchball. Stairball.

A few months into the season, we went to a soccer camp in Hazlet, New Jersey. We played a few games against some local teams from that area. Our team was shitty. The teams from Hazlet were really good. A large percentage of the people living in that area were first and second-generation Irish, Scottish, Welsh, and English. They took the game very seriously. Soccer was part of their culture. There were a thousand people watching us play. It was a little scary. We were lucky if we got thirty fans to watch us play in Bridgewater.

In the first game, we were totally outclassed. There must have been about seven or eight breakaways and three or four penalty shots. I stopped all but two of the breakaways by ranging way out of the net and tackling the attacking player. I let in two of the four penalty shots. I thought I played OK, but not brilliantly, and I was disgusted that we lost four to one.

After the match, I was hanging my head, feeling very shy, and sitting in the school cafeteria. This was my first time away from home without my parents, and I felt totally weirded out. Although, the Irish family that put me up for the weekend was lovely, sweet, and fun.

As I ate my lunch, the tall, thin, rugged-looking Scot who reffed our match snuck up beside me and started talking nose-to-nose in a really shrill manner.

"All of the scouts here have agreed that you are the best under sixteen goalkeeper they have ever seen."

I was ignoring him, because I was weirded out by being away from home, and because I didn't really like soccer that much at the time.

"Look at me when I'm talking to ya. There are about six or seven high school coaches here who would like you to play for them when you start ninth grade. The supporter club will fly you out at your convenience, and you can visit the schools and decide where you'd like to play."

"Thank you, but I don't know if I like soccer or not."

"That's all right. Give it a chance. We figure after high school we can get you a college scholarship in the UK or Ireland, unless a team wants you at eighteen. We figure you would start at division III in England or Ireland. After that, it depends how you answer to the pressure. The press. The fans.

"I don't know what to say. I don't really like soccer, to be honest."

"To tell you the truth, a lot of the professional players don't like football that much, anymore. The fans take the game so seriously that they drive everyone mad. I know that in the States, football is shite. But in Europe, it's quite a different matter. Your money is no good anywhere. Pubs. Restaurants. Nightclubs. And you have to fight the birds off with a stick. Look at that bird."

The Scot pointed to a beautiful blond lady of about thirty-seven. Think Susan George.

"That's my wife. Take a good look at her, it's OK. If she leaves me, there's ten more just like her. That's a footballer's life, mate."

I told the Scot that I would think about it and thanked him very much for his offer. He said the offer was good for three years.

And one of those scouts contacted me every six months or so to see if I would come out to New Jersey to visit the schools. Well, at fifty-two, I'm ready to start playing. It is only at this time that I have developed the tranquility to handle such pressure. In fact, I spend a good deal of time trading currencies, so I haven't avoided activities that are pressure-packed. It was just, at twelve years of age, I couldn't commit to a pressure-cooker situation in an activity I didn't love. If I had three lives to live, one of them would have included moving away to another high school to be a soccer player. Sometimes I think I should have spent this life doing just that. I would have avoided a lot of madness at home, but it was just too big of a change for me. Ironically, I played American football for three years, even though I didn't like it, just to be popular. I could have been quite popular in New Jersey just by playing soccer well. So, that's how stupid I am.

THE ARMY AND ME

Soon after I graduated high school, I was in the army for a short spell. I met a lot of nice people there. But, ultimately, the US Army just wasn't sympathetic to my caffeine needs. Sure, coffee was served at breakfast, lunch, and dinner. Great plastic thermoses of coffee were also trucked to work details along the roadsides for breaks. However, at this time of my life, I needed several more coffee breaks, especially at night. Fortunately, I met a friend in the army, Kenny Loony, who found that the US Army wasn't fully sympathetic to his tobacco needs. Sure, the army allowed many tobacco breaks to Kenny during the day, but Kenny needed several more, because tobacco was Kenny's thing.

The only things that Kenny would ever say were, "Where you from, my man, DC? Salid. The City? Salid," or "Hey, my man, you gut a cigarette?"

But since most soldiers smoked their smokes when they had them, Kenny had to devise other means to feed his ravenous tobacco jones. Hence, Kenny and I took to going to the other side of the base for cigs at the PX and coffee at the coffee machine nearby.

At first, I was hesitant, but Kenny would always be like, "It's cool, man. I don't wanna go alone. If two guys go, we won't get hassled."

So, I always went with Kenny, since I did need my coffee. We always got hassled, though. Some fucking sergeant or other would always sneak up behind us double-time and yell into our ears, "What are you two doing here? State your business!"

And Kenny would calmly explain some complete bullshit about us delivering a message to some made-up sergeant. I always thought we would get caught and get in big trouble, but we always got away with it. I marveled at our success. Kenny explained, "Shit, this army can't outthink a bunch of peasants in sandals. Ain't no big thing."

As for the drill sergeants, many of them were actually pretty nice people. I especially liked many of the black drill sergeants. They put on this act of saying they wanted to rip off our heads and skull fuck us, but they were actually very caring and kind. The few white drill sergeants were nasty fucks, though. They wouldn't threaten to anally rape us, but they would often fine you or send a poor soldier to military adjustment units, which were nasty places. I could see how some of those bastards could get themselves fragged in wartime, because they were such fuckheads. And that is a no-shitter.

The assistant drill sergeant of our platoon was a black guy, but he was sort of a pain in the ass. He would explain how to use a weapon very quickly. And then when someone asked for them to explain it more slowly, the sergeant would instead speed up the demonstration to confuse the hapless soldier even more. One time this sergeant pulled this routine in explaining how to open up a light anti-tank weapon. This weapon was basically a plastic tube with a few pieces that flipped up and down. Sergeant Washington's sarcastic attitude and yelling really pissed me the fuck off, so I called the motherfucker out. I got nose-to-nose with the man and started screaming at him, "Negative reinforcement doesn't fucking work! You idiots barely fucking beat the South with a three-to-one advantage in manpower. Couldn't fucking beat the Koreans. lost in fucking Vietnam to a bunch of fucking starving peasants!"

I was hoping we would either have a good fight, or I would get punched out and sue the army, but Sergeant Washington just laughed. I saw the pupils in his eyes bulge in and out, like muscles on a big, strong guy.

"Ha. That's some good shit, Private Dee." And then he walked off to bust out some other hapless bastard.

I really enjoyed all the rifle instruction and practice in the army. We must have shot several thousand rounds in the six weeks I was in basic training. I had some trouble hitting the bull's-eye, though, so I was given extra instruction by an expert rifle instructor. And I got better, too. I still remember those lessons.

I also had trouble making my bed perfectly, as the army requested.

I could never get those corner sheet folds to display that nice diagonal fold, so cherished by this man's army. So, I traded services with a few of the guys in the platoon.

They took turns making my bed perfectly, while I showed them how to remember all the items in their army code of conduct manual that we would be tested on. I used pneumonic memory shit like making an acronym out of the six items they needed to remember for one topic. For instance, one was FLIFPIM. Each letter stood for one answer in the category. At first, the guys thought I was full of shit and just scamming on their beautiful bed-making skills. I had to guarantee them that they would pass their test using my methods, or I would pay them five dollars each for every week they made my bed. They expected to get paid right up until they took their test, which of course they passed with very high grades.

Kenny and I were kicked out of the army soon after this episode. The army officially ruled that they could not fully honor our caffeine and tobacco needs. The last time I saw Kenny was when we rode the bus north together. Kenny got off the bus in Pittsburgh. He didn't say much to me. Just, "So long." Then he nodded his head as he always did and gave me this stare of recognition, as if to say, "Well, that's life. Sort of weird, sort of enjoyable."

I used to have that type of relationship with a guy in high school named Pete Flanagan. I would usually see Pete only at parties, because we were in different classes. It would usually be late into the party, when people were dancing and yelling. A few guys would be staggering around telling people that they weren't drunk. That's about the time really silly things would happen. One time I tried to take a pee in a bathroom and found the toilet clogged with puke. Just as I discovered that the bathroom lacked a plunger to unclog the toilet, Pete arrived to take a pee, quickly assessed the situation, and shook his head with a gleam in his eye.

Another time, Pete and I were sitting at a table sipping crappy Busch beer and listening to five slurred, illogical, drunken discussions that were overlapping. I think Blue Oyster Cult's "Don't Fear the Reaper" was playing for the six-thousandth time. We then saw a crowd gather in the kitchen next to the living room. When we joined the crowd to discover the cause of the ruckus, we saw an acquaintance's elder sister lying on the kitchen table, joyously accepting a fuck with a pool cue. I mean she was screaming like mad out of joy. Pete and I immediately exchanged nods and gleams of the eye. Wonderful, terrible, sad, joyous, unpredictable. 'Tis. As the Irish say.

And no police. No SWAT teams. And no bitch from social services.

MORE FLORA AND FAUNA

When I left high school and went into the world, I met a lot of strange people. One of them was Barry Fleischman. I met Barry when I moved into a house with three other people in Boulder, Colorado. Barry dressed all in black. He had a Mohawk that was always covered by a black baseball cap and adorned with a red Chairman Mao pin. Barry had a job as a library guard at the local university. Barry would punch in on the time clock at the library and then go to a movie or go home to read Karl Marx.

Whenever I got home from work at my job as a prep cook at the Failing Fern Bar, Barry would harangue me about the plight of the worker and how I should rise up and smote my oppressors. I was actually OK with the capitalist system, but I thought it needed to be fine-tuned some. I was into the stock market and stock options. In the beginning of October 1987, I thought the stock market might crash. I probably thought this when all of the financial news pundits were saying that the future was fabulous. That's always a warning sign. Anyway, for some reason I got Barry interested in stock options. I told him we should buy some put options that day. With put options, you make money when the stock goes down.

Well, despite being a declared communist, Barry was above all very impressionable. So, before you know it, we were both filling out brokerage applications at the old Fred Bonnell brokerage on Arapahoe Avenue in Boulder. Sort of an old-school place with a bunch of dazed old-timers milling around trying to trade off of rumors and bits of disinformation. Into this scene comes Barry with his Mohawk and black SWAT gear, swearing on his application that he was worth three million dollars and had five years of experience trading stock options. Fred's expression was like, "What the fuck?" But as long as Barry swore he knew what he was doing, Fred wouldn't be held accountable for Barry's likely loss of money.

So, Barry and I bought four Federal Express ninety-dollar put options that expired in three months. The options cost five dollars a share times the four hundred shares. Each option was for one hundred shares. Federal Express was selling for like ninety-eight dollars a share. A put option gives the buyer the right but not the obligation to sell a given stock at a given price by a given time. We were at the brokerage on a Friday. It was still the old days of stock trading, so we didn't have to put up any money until three business days after our purchase. But on the following Monday, wouldn't you know it, the stock market crashed.

Federal Express stock fell from ninety-eight to about sixty-three dollars per share. So, we made twenty-seven dollars a share, because each put option gave us the right to sell one hundred shares of Federal Express at ninety dollars. So, we made almost twelve thousand dollars in three days without putting up a dime. This is the absolute truth. This is Dee talking. And I ain't lying.

So, about a week later, I came home from work, dirty and sweaty. As usual, Barry was luxuriating on the couch and reading his communist feces. When Barry saw me, he jumped off the couch and started reading from Marx: "And the workers of the world must unite! They must organize into unions. They must organize into party cadres. The workers of the worlds must recognize their class… wait a minute, I forgot to call my stockbroker."

Another classic Barry Fleischman move concerned our other room-mate, Tony Gonzalez. Tony lived in a makeshift bedroom downstairs that we made using curtains for walls. Tony's bedroom allowed us to cram five people into our eight hundred-dollar-a-month house, thereby dropping the rent to one hundred sixty dollars per month per person.

Anyway, Tony was often in his curtain room making it with his cute girlfriend, Raquel. Tony would order a pizza right before boinking his girlfriend and then forget about it before getting down to business. So, when the pizza delivery guy would show up with the pie, Barry would pay for the pizza, go downstairs, and open the curtains to Tony's room and watch the performers doing their thing.

After about five minutes, Raquel would notice the voyeur and yell, "Barry! What are you doing, man!"

According to Raquel, Barry would have this wistful, longing expression on his face like he was this old man reminiscing about his own good times as he watched Tony and Raquel fucking. Barry was only twenty-five at the time.

Barry would then announce, all innocent-like, "Pizza's here!"

Another time, Barry was making a Thai green curry. So, when he decided to go downstairs and watch the Tony and Raquel Show, he announced loudly, "Has anyone seen my Kaffir leaves!"

Another crazy person I met in Boulder was Jack Swackhammer. I met Jack when I was manning the hamburger station at Burger King. Swack was this stocky, hairy dude with thick eyeglasses and an intense stare. He was a high school student at the Fire and Brimstone School of Certain Eternal Damnation. The first shift I worked with Swack, he was having a tough day. Swack was manning the fry area. He listened for orders of whaler fish sandwiches and chicken filet sandwiches and then prepared them. That day those orders were coming in hot and heavy.

"Whaler. Whaler. Two whalers. Chicken san. Chicken san, no lettuce. Whaler, no tartar. Two chicken san, no mayo. Whaler. Whaler. Whaler, no lettuce. One chicken san, no lettuce, no mayo, no bun. Whaler. Whaler."

After this barrage of orders, Swack took matters into his own hands. He manned the barricades. In quick order, he turned off all the fryolaters. He turned off the meat and bun warmers. Then he made a sign that read: "This Side Closed Till Further Notice."

Cecile, the speedy cheese side burger area worker, ignored the sign and informed Swack, "The chicken san, no lettuce, no mayo, no bun is for that nice old lady over there in the flower hat. Well, it's for her poodle, Herschel."

Cecile motioned over to the lady, whose two-dollar "Evening in Detroit" perfume was nauseating.

Swack looked at the lady and yelled, "Fuck Herschel! We should serve fried Herschel sandwiches!"

The manager was this sweet, hardworking Latino dude named Roberto. Roberto walked over to Swack and told him to calm down. Roberto then started making the sandwiches.

At this point, I figured Swack was a pretty amusing character, so I introduced myself.

"Always eat your fiber. Have you ever seen a rabbit with hemorrhoids?"

Swack stared at me blankly for a long time. Then he started working on the backload of sandwich orders with Roberto. I guess he figured he'd rather make fifty greasy fish sandwiches than listen to my warpage.

A few years later, Swack worked as a construction foreman for a roofing company in Tokyo, Japan. One night when Swack was representing all over the local talent at a nearby brothel, he noticed that some of his American countryman were acting out in an awful way downstairs in the lobby. The misbehaving Yanks were throwing chairs and beer bottles, as well as talking trash to the mama-san. So, Swack being Swack, he busted a few skulls and restored order to that happy house of lust tout de suite. Well, mama-san was very grateful and called up the Yakuza owners of the house to report how Swack had saved the situation. Next thing you know, Swack is going out on calls with the Yakuza collecting debts and busting heads. The Yakuza guys even did a mock mixing of blood from the fingers ceremony. Unfortunately for Swack, the Yakuza told him he couldn't really be a member of the Yakuza, because he wasn't Japanese.

I went to Japan a few years later. Tokyo. Loved the people. Delicious food. Very cool police. We would sit and drink beer on the sidewalk of our house at two in the morning every day. The police would come by and chat. Very sweet. And the women were dead sexy. And they dressed to please. None of this hippie feces.

Swack was also a great video game player. He could last thirty minutes on one quarter, easy. When Swack was working at a local dry cleaner, he embezzled twenty-five thousand dollars over the course of two years and used the money to perfect his touch on the joystick.

Swack then became one of the bigger marijuana dealers in town. One time the police were called to Swack's apartment by a neighbor who suspected he was a drug dealer. But when the police came to Swack's apartment, they recognized him as an acquaintance who went to many of the same parties they did. So, the cops just stole his pound of weed and eight hundred dollars and called it even stephen.

Swack used to sell many pounds of weed per week to the city gangs.

A few times I accompanied him on these rounds. The delivery spot was a nondescript apartment building. The atmosphere was very casual. The scene looked like four college kids hanging out in the afternoon after class. It was a couple of white and black and Asian kids. A very professional operation. No gangbangers hanging out threatening people, or the like.

It was amazing to think what a cross section of humanity Swack would sell his weed to. We would go visit kindly old grannies working in coffee shops and drop off a pound. Then we'd pop into a ritzy downtown office building and deliver two pounds of primo kick-ass weed to some smooth-looking master-of-the-universe type. Fun times. Then another pound to some soccer mom working at a kiddie toy store.

One time Swack called me from one of the phone booths that used to line the pedestrian mall in town. He went on this thirty-minute crying jag about how he was through with women. From then on, it would only be porn and prostitutes. Or he would go gay. In the middle of this wallowing in self-warpage, he meets a girl he hadn't seen in two years. Of course, he makes a date with the girl and hangs up.

Another time, I was hanging out at Swack's apartment. He said he was on a health kick and was only eating chicken and vegetables. So, I went into his freezer to grab a piece of chicken to cook, but the chicken was only half-wrapped and had major freezer burn. Maybe thirty slices, all completely wasted. I told Swack. He got pissed-off and started throwing the chicken pieces out of his fourth-floor window toward the Dumpster about a hundred feet away. He missed every time. After a while, a black guy sitting on a third-floor balcony of a neighboring apartment yelled, "Hey, man! Show the neighborhood some respect!"

Swack eyed the man savagely and yelled, "Black people are always causing trouble in this neighborhood!"

I also became pen pals with the leader of a cargo cult. I had read about this guy, Tom Melies, who headed up a cargo cult in Vanuatu. So, I just had to write him to say hello and send him some cargo.

MY LIFE WITH THE CARGO CULT

Cargo cults came about during World War II when Allied armies arrived on Pacific Islands that hadn't seen Western culture with all their fancy, complicated shit. When the Allies took over an island for the duration, they brought canned food and telephones and planes and cars and bicycles and motorcycles and radios and just so much magical shit that the natives figured that these guys must be gods. So, the natives started worshipping the leader of these occupational forces as a god and expected his return. Sounds familiar, huh?

So, anyway, I sent John a bunch of cargo like silver ingots, combs, US postage, and a letter telling John that a lot of people in the West were really members of cargo cults, too, they just didn't know it.

John wrote back a nice letter inviting me to visit him on Vanuatu and agreeing that many people are worshippers in cargo cults and don't know it. I sure would like some nice stuff. Like a Tesla sedan and a big house.

BOULDER, COLORADO

I've lived in Boulder, Colorado for twenty-six years. The weather is pleasant. A lot of energy. And there are some interesting, good people here. Especially the software engineers. Lately, however, a bunch of pushy, annoying East Coasters have moved here—yuck.

I lived in a commune for three years. Actually, it stopped being a commune after about six months, because these things are about people being groovy and kind, and people just aren't that groovy and kind. Anyway, the leader of the commune was this eighty-seven-year-old guy with Parkinson's called Jack. Jack used to be very athletic and was into skiing and hiking and biking. By the time I met him, Jack was spending a lot of time utilizing his walker to creep around the house nude and watching free porn on the computer into the wee hours. Jack would often walk in ultra-slow motion downstairs to the room of another roommate, Mycroft, a computer genius. Jack would knock on Mycroft's door for about twenty minutes until he woke the gifted, yet sleepy, genius. Jack would then motion upstairs till Mycroft followed him to discover the problem. Invariably, the computer would be frozen onto some lewd double-anal porn scene. Frozen because Dick had once again spilled his smoothie onto the keyboard.

TRAVELING MAN: LONDON

Like I said, I have had some time away from Boulder for good behavior. I spent six months in London in 1999 working as a security guard at the Funky International School. I also took some classes in diplomacy there. That school was a pretty crazy place.

A typical security guard shift on the weekends consisted of me staggering into the guardroom at seven in the morning. The room was located at the back of the front lobby. Five minutes later, my French friend, Guy, would arrive with two six-packs of warm Heineken. Guy would spend the next two hours bitching about the United States and filling up the tiny guardroom with two packs of Marlboro smoke.

At eight, my girlfriend, Jolee, would arrive. She would sit on my lap and say nothing. She would also add about another pack of Marlboro smoke to the festivities. At about nine, Mateuz, my friend from Slovenia, would arrive. He would echo Guy's criticisms of the United States, along with adding about a pack and a half of smoke to our tiny party hut.

The only people coming and going at that hour on the weekends were the Eastern European drug lord students and the local dealers to whom they dealt. Since these drug lords didn't sell heroin, only pills and weed, I didn't call the cops on the QT. Those guys were pleasant to chat with. We usually talked about soccer-related gossip.

After a few hours on my weekend shift, something weird would always happen. One time an Indian student on the second floor jizzed out a window onto a Pakistani student who was standing outside, two stories down. The Pakistani guy stormed past the guardroom, posse in tow, and bounded up the stairs to the second floor. I could barely make out what the fuck was up, as the guardroom was so smoky after three hours of Mateuz, Guy, and Jolee puffing away that it looked like a Kiss concert. I did hear the Pakistani kid screaming, "You threw dirty water on me! You threw dirty water on me! I kill you! I kill you!"

I could vaguely hear some dustup going on, but I wasn't about to get involved with that shit. I was making like four pounds per hour, for Christ's fucking sake.

One time, during my security shift, all three of us sat on the steps in front of the school and just watched all the weird people go by. Waterloo was a pretty piss-poor part of London, full of nutbags. It took us all of ten minutes to spy a tall, muscular man with crazed hair who was walking down the middle of York Street, peeing on the streets as he went. That guy must have drunk about ten pints of beer, because it was a really long pee. Meanwhile, this young blond kid of about fifteen was following this guy down the street and videotaping the action.

A few moments later, two big guys emerged, swearing, from their cars parked in the middle of the road. But one of the big guys quickly realized that the other guy was a lot bigger. So, this smaller guy escapes by jumping the sidewalk railing to put a barrier between himself and the bigger guy. Then the bigger guy jumps over the railing to get the other guy, uttering foul oaths along the way.

"I'll cripple you, mate!"

"So, you're a big fucking man!"

Then the smaller guy jumped back to his original side of the railing screaming, "You're a right bastard, you are!"

This scene went on a full ten minutes before both combatants tired out, shook hands, and departed in their respective cars.

As a break from this mad theater, I would often grab a fried ham and egg sandwich and large hot tea from Benjy's, a sandwich shop on the Strand. I would then chill out on a bench at the nearby Embankment Park. I used to meet this nice old queen every day, a retired bookkeeper. Very sweet man. He told me that only about 2 percent of London was swinging in the sixties. I met often this big

Cuban guy who said that he was on the run from Castro's assassins. He took me to this Brazilian dance club in Leicester Square near the Prince Charles Theater. Brazilian dance club: festive, fun. Prince Charles Theater: midnight matinee is two pounds. Good fun and full of nutters.

As for Guy, he would take the tube from pub to pub, consuming perhaps twenty pints of beer per day. He always sat at a window to be on the lookout for any of his many acquaintances. If he saw one, he would run onto the sidewalk, sliding on the shiny soles of his dress shoes, wheedling, "Let's go to zee pub."

Once in the pub, Guy would harangue the startled acquaintance for the better part of an hour about the greatness of France and French culture and how the English and Americans were trash.

One of my bosses at my guard job was a real loon. He was this thirty-year-old Brit named Lionel. Every couple of weeks, he would get a package in the mail that included some cash. I was supposed to give the package to Lionel after work at five. Otherwise, Lionel would take the cash, buy a pint of whiskey, and hightail it to the Soho stroke booths while on the clock. So, of course, I always forgot my instructions from the big boss and gave Lionel the package right away. And then it was my task to go to every stroke shop in Soho and find Lionel. And I had to bang on every stroke booth in the shops to find the freak. One time, one of the guys in the booth asked if he could suck my ass.

"I'm on the clock," I protested.

"Even better," He cajoled.

This degree program in diplomacy amounted to another opportunity missed. It was a one-year degree consisting of twelve classes, six per semester. I was told by one professor that if I finished the program, I could get a job with the US Department of State. However, I wasn't quite interested enough in diplomacy to pursue this opportunity.

As a student at Schiller, we always got invited to these boozy diplomatic receptions. And we were always late. And I usually had my fly down when I showed up at the embassy. One time, the Ecuadorian ambassador motioned toward my downed fly as he poured me a cup of coffee.

At one reception at the Canadian embassy, I remember a diplomat from Rwanda telling me that the massacres there weren't as bad as the newspapers portrayed and that the journalists were always blowing things out of proportion and ruining tourism.

Along that note, one of my diplomacy professors had been a hostage during the Iran Hostage Crisis. He said that his captors were very nice and that the newspapers made the situation seem a lot more dangerous than it was. The professor also added that he won a bunch of money playing poker with his captors

We did a lot of the usual tourist stuff in London—the White Tower, parliament building, Royal Haymarket Theatre, concerts at St. Martin-in-the-Fields, the National Portrait Gallery, the British Museum, the Clink, Buckingham Palace, Windsor Palace, eel pie shops, tea at Harrods, tea at the Pump Room in Bath, etc. Interesting. Often impressive. But it's never a first-time experience one gets with tourist attractions nowadays, as one sees them first in books and TV, and one receives the opinions of others concerning these attractions before one can formulate one's own take.

Therefore, I must say that I get more of a feel for a place by riding around the buses and subways and eating at working man's cafes than by doing the tourist thing. For one thing, many of the Brits display a theatrical air. When I first arrived at Heathrow and was taking the escalator between the airport and the subway, I heard someone screeching. It was a big woman all in leather who was a double for Ozzy Osbourne. She was reciting a parody of the famous Spice Girls song. "Tell ya what I want! Tell ya what I want! What I really, really want! What I really, really fucking want…is a good man! That's all I fuckin' want! And I ask you girls…is that too much to fuckin' ask!

Cue: mad cheering by about five hundred women of various ages and classes.

And another thing: the British women are dead sexy and dress to please. None of this hippie shit.

PARIS

When I went to Paris with Mateuz on import-export business, we hung out with Guy, who lived there. Mateuz and I enjoyed the museums like the Louvre and the military museum. We also loved walking the neighborhoods and smelling the delicious food items that were for sale on the street. Like the roast quails and the chestnuts. The whole time we were in Paris, Guy insisted on dragging us to at least a dozen pubs and porn shops. When Guy's Muslim brother-in-law was in town, Guy dragged him into a porn shop in Les Halles and made him look at scat porn, where both lovers were covered in what looked like chocolate as they screwed. Guy's staid brother-in-law let out this long, loud, high-pitched titter as he looked at the magazine in disbelief.

Another time, Guy and I were walking in a quieter quarter of Paris. At an intersection, a young guy on a scooter was so intent on gazing upon this beautiful brunette woman with long, silky hair and great legs clad in a black leather miniskirt that he drove right through a red light. To save his skin from the oncoming traffic, the scooter guy then needed to drive into several tables on the sidewalk of a cafe, ditching his bike in the process. The damage: Two overturned tables, four meals dumped onto the ground. One waiter down, along with his dropped tray and broken ceramic dishes. One scratched-up scooter and a scooter guy with one case of serious road rash.

A police officer was immediately on the scene and heard the screaming testimony of both the waiter and the owner of the cafe.

"Idiot! He must pay. The fool."

"She was pretty, what can I say?"

The police officer surveyed the damage for a full minute. Then he ruled: "There wasn't much damage. We're all men here. These things happen."

The police officer then walked on. And so did Mateuz and I, to the serenading screams of the owner still batshit pissed-off at the scooter guy.

If this happened in the United States, there would have been the SWAT team, four police cars, an ambulance, a fire truck, three lawyers, and that bitch from social services.

Another time, Guy took us on the TGV fast train from Paris to Bordeaux. Of course, Guy dragged us to the pub car where we stayed for the duration. But even at one hundred and fifty mph, the French countryside looked lovely with its green fields and stately brown and decaying chateaus. It really didn't seem like we were going so fast, except when we would accelerate after a slowdown, and the bartender would give up on the espresso he was making, laugh, and say, "Fuck it." At that moment, the *g* forces were kicking my ass to the bowels of the earth.

Anyway, Guy took us to this lush and large vineyard that had acres of tiny champagne grapes. I jumped in and nibbled several bunches of these cuties. So sweet. Lovely flavor. Soon, though, these vineyard workers appeared and told us to please stop eating the grapes, because the harvest hadn't taken place yet. After the harvest, we could come back and nibble to our satisfaction.

Guy, however, was unperturbed. "Comrades," began Guy, all liberty, fraternity, and equality-like. "This vineyard has been controlled by my family since 1464."

"What's your name?" asked one worker, cordially.

"Guy de Marthon," declared Guy, proudly. With a bit less of the liberty, fraternity, and equality thingy.

"But, monsieur, that vineyard is three kilometers to the south. This vineyard is owned by a convent."

So, file this affair under *W* for WTF?

And then, later in the day, Guy insisted that we go to this wine tasting at this other chateau a few miles away from the site of his last embarrassment. And boy did we get all blotto, and I mean swacked and feeling no pain. I didn't know that Bordeaux wine could taste that good. So fruity and balanced. And not tart. But we tasted fifty-dollar Bordeaux, not the seven-dollar liquefied funk at the local packy that usually infests our local dos.

Anyway, after leaving the wine tasting, Guy and Mateuz forgot how to get back to our hotel in Bordeaux. This was especially amusing as Guy had lived in Bordeaux for thirty years. This state of affairs was also disconcerting because Mateuz was blaring Duran Duran's greatest hits album over and over on the stereo. I like the band, but the tales of excess were adding too comical a tone to our proceedings, in addition to impairing my ability to think.

We kept passing this crew of Albanian prostitutes who kept laughing at us for being so lost. Finally, Mateuz stopped the car and told Guy to ask the Joy Division for directions back to the hotel. It was almost three in the morning, and Guy wanted to get back before the bar closed in an hour. So, what happened? The prostitutes demanded we give them all a ride back to their hotel before they gave us instructions to ours. And Guy, Mateuz, and I were already cramped in a fucking Fiat Punto. So, in came the three prosties on our laps. And wouldn't you know it, but the one on Guy's lap started giving him a hand job. I could tell, because he gave off this effete Gallic wheeze whenever he was being pleasured. (I lived next door to him, and the walls were thin.)

Just as I was luxuriating in the warpage of this orgy in an Italian cat food can, we got stopped by the cops.

"What's going on here, monsieurs?" they asked, laughing as they saw the prosties on our laps, but stopped as they smelled the fine Boudreaux on our collective breaths.

"We got lost from the vineyard. Can you give us directions back to the hotel?" said Guy, conspiratorially with the gendarmes. He included something like, "We are all Europeans here, and boys will be boys, and we know the score... except for Dee, who is an uptight American."

Fortunately, the cops just laughed and agreed and gave the whole crew an escort to the prostie hotel and the three boys an escort to their hotel.

And then we got back to our hotel in Les Halles and watched a French chat show, and whose song, "Stop Your Bitching," is the theme song of the fuckin' show? Caroline's band, Big Soul, that's who.

FLORIDA

I spent a year and a half in Sarasota, Florida, from the fall of 1984 to the spring of 1986. I liked the people in Florida. I liked the white people. I liked the black people. I liked the old-timers. I spent many fun afternoons in coffee shops talking baseball with the old boys. I liked the pretty beaches on Lido Key and Saint Armand's, but I could not stand the heat and humidity in Florida. It was oppressive. It depressed me. So, in the spring of '86, it was "Exit, Stage West" to Colorado.

I spent the summer of 1982 in Berkeley, California. Pallone and I rented a room in a frat house for forty dollars per month each. The weather in Berkeley was a revelation. It was cool all summer. Loved it. I worked stuffing envelopes with a crew of lovable, crazy people. One kid from Kansas aspired to be a porn film critic. He was always going on about the aesthetic craft displayed in the work of John Holmes and Ron Jeremy. All this porn talk set off this other kid, who wouldn't stop saying, "Man, I gut the length. I always gut the length."

I just loved hanging out on Telegraph Avenue, munching a huge one-dollar slice of Blondie's Pizza and taking in all the warpage, including word salad guys, who would walk hurriedly up and down the sidewalk spewing whatever headline came into their head: Vietnam! Social Stratification! Queer Theory! Colonialism! Manifest Destiny!"

And there was this young lady who was always dancing ballet in a nightgown and golden slippers.

We used to hang out with Pallone's roommate from Stanford, Mitch O'Brian. Mitch was a sweet, generous, funny, lovely person. But he did have this impish leprechaun's taste for practical jokes. One time we all had dinner at Mitch's parents place in San Rafael, Marin County. The other guest at dinner was Mitch's cousin Barry, who was a Catholic priest in the Republic of Ireland. As soon as Father Barry shook my hand in greeting, Mitch announced that I thought the

Brits were doing a great job in Northern Ireland. Now, I never said any such thing. That situation is none of my damn business.

Anyway, when Father Barry heard this statement, he went batshit. "I'm not eating with this fucking bastard! Are you taking the piss, Mitch, inviting this black-and-tan trash to sup with the family?" With that, Father Barry stormed off.

I was in a Royalist phase at this time, but I never said anything about the situation in Northern Ireland. Maybe I should have, because my dad's side of the family emigrated from Northern Ireland to North Carolina in the 1740s.

Anyway, one afternoon I got really drunk on Night Train wine and wandered around downtown Berkeley. I ended up sitting on the curb barfing. A couple of police officers asked if I was OK and drove me home. They were very sweet and caring. I love the police. If it wasn't for the cops, we would all be constantly riding posse in cycles of revenge, like in the old days. The police, fire, medical personnel, and educators. God's chosen few. The real superstars. Accept no imitations.

When the police brought me upstairs, I told them that they didn't have to worry about me, because I was a Royalist. That cracked up the cops and also the group of frat guys who came out of their rooms to check out the ruckus. They invited me to join their frat on the spot. I was honored, but I told them I wasn't a student at Berkeley but Occidental College in Los Angeles.

I worked in a sub shop on Alameda owned by this sweet Cambodian guy. He had one fault, though. Every time a transvestite came into the shop, he would start to crack up and run into his office. As I tried to be casual and ask the customer which sandwich he/she would like, we would hear maniacal cackling coming from the office. Since Berkeley had a lot of transvestites, this cackling caper happened about twice a week.

I spent the next summer in Marin County, California. Specifically, the laid-back town of sunny San Rafael. I spent a mellow time hanging out with Mitch's family and working part-time in a grocery store.

My other task was to help Mitch's brother, Max the Coke Dealer, sample every weekly shipment of marching powder.

"If you guys are gonna be hanging around all the time, the least you can do is help me test this shit."

Max said that his nose was getting too screwed up to keep testing the shit. Max made about one thousand a week profit from selling it. I thought the stuff was OK. It gave me a happy lift, but I wouldn't blow money on it unless I was making a ton of dough at a high-pressure job, like a stock broker.

As for Max, he said he would give up selling the coke after he was arrested once. True to his word, Max was arrested about four years later and promptly gave up his sales career, just as he promised the judge. Except that Max is still dealing, only this time it's real estate. So, Max is still selling dreams.

HELD-UP AT GUNPOINT

When I was nineteen, I was still living at home. I went to the local state college for two years and worked at a local store in East Bridgewater. One afternoon, this short, skinny guy with dark hair came in and pulled a gun and said, "Give me the all the money, or I'm gonna smash you!"

I thought he was kidding and told him politely not to joke about things like that. Then the guy got really mad and said, "I'm gonna fuckin' smash you if you don't give me the money now!"

"OK, you got it," I said, my heart racing wildly. I opened the cash register and put all the cash on the counter.

"Hurry up, or I'll smash you."

"Here, take the money."

It was a game that I got stuck playing, and I just wanted it to end. The guy had a crazy, impatient look on his face, like he was on some shit.

"Hurry up!" the guy yelled. I thought he might shoot me anyway. In my fright, I was still thinking of strategies. I decided that if he looked like he was going to shoot me, I would stick my left hand over the barrel of the gun, taking the bullet in my hand. Then I would gouge out his left eye with my right hand.

It didn't come to that, because the freak took the money and left. The police were very nice, but they did take me to the station and have me tell them the whole story three or four times. Then I had to write the whole story down three or four times. Then I had to work with the guy that does a mock up of the perp based on individual facial features on transparencies.

For about two months after this scare, I felt numb and depressed. As I often felt growing up in my parents' house when they were having their rows. Numbness is a tactic that I often used to get through sad and depressing times. The problem with using numbness is that it's hard to turn on and turn off at will. So, I have spent my life avoiding pain and the possibility of pain. And therefore, I have spent my life in a state of numbness. Usually, when I have had the chance at an enriching life experiences that contained potential pain, I would avoid that experience. For this reason, I have never wanted to have a pet, even though I have loved many of my friends' pets. And for this reason, I have only had a few girlfriends.

So, I would suggest to today's "utes" to spend less time getting numb and more time picking an interest and pursuing it. Pursuing that interest up to the point that they can make a living at it. Don't spend your life working shitty restaurant jobs, as I have.

Why, one time, I was at the now defunct Joe and Nemo's sub shop at the old Boston Garden. It was right after the lunch rush, and I ordered a meatball sandwich and watched one of the cooks just go bananas. Screaming, yelling, throwing dishes. Then he glared at me.

"I'll just have a slice of pizza," I offered in a gesture of peace.

I guess this guy had had his fill of making sandwiches that day.

Just then, another guy comes over and says, "No, have your sandwich."

He then got in the cook's face and yelled, "Make the sandwich, or get out of here. You're here to work."

And the guy started making the sandwich. But then he turned to me, more calmly, and said, "Don't waste your life working shit jobs like this. Find something you like to do, and make money with it."

I didn't think much of that incident until recently, because I thought I would never be like that person. Of course, I became that person.

SEX AND KIDS AT YALE

I was on the debate team at school. We took a field trip every year to a different Model UN. One year we went to the New York Model UN. We visited the real UN and saw the American and Soviet delegates vilifying each other at a meeting of the Economic and Social Council. We were staying at a swanky hotel and went to a bunch of parties and drank a lot. One night, our group drunkenly got into an elevator, and who did we see? Both the American and Soviet delegates drunk as skunks, hugging each other and laughing. So, don't believe everything we were taught, kids.

At the Yale Model UN the next year, we were drunk as skunks the entire time. One afternoon, Jimmy V and I went for a walk on the snowy Yale campus. Jimmy V was this nutbag who had a weird sense of humor that included talking with a British accent and driving on the left side of the road at odd moments. After about ten minutes, we fell in with a couple of cute brunettes. These girls had pints of vodka on them. So, we were all soon drunker than the fleet. At some point, we paired off and had some kind of sex. Don't remember exactly if I was stroked off or if there was some petite penetration. I do remember that it was with one of the girls, though. Jimmy V was with the other chick.

I also remember getting into drunken pig piles with Mr. Gaspari, our advisor. He took it in stride. But, as he was always smoking a cigar, he would yell, "Watch my Antony and Cleopatra. These are fuckin' expensive!"

LESSONS LEARNED?

My old Mac mini-computer is starting to fuck up, so I will end this collection of tales here. As for a moral to this shit, there isn't one. I have learned that is important to eat a lot of fiber every day. William Demarest was so right. Being in pain after every shit is a crappy way to go through life.

I've also learned that numbness is a very expensive way to deal with pain. But I don't know any other way. I should see a psychiatrist. I did see a psychiatrist, once.

I was working in the Career Library at the University of Colorado. The school psychologists had offices at the other end of the same building. Carly was a fiftyish brunette with cat's eye glasses and a bouffant hairdo. She was doing a six-month stretch in a wheelchair due to a wreck. Every day at lunch, she would wheel her sorry ass into our library and munch down her tuna san with our crew. Carly ate with us to avoid trucking it through the throng of thirty-five thousand deeply serious scholars at the university.

One afternoon, as Carly was rolling in for lunch, I asked her for one of the psychology sessions due to me per year (one of six) as a student.

"Here's my biggest problem," I began. "I grew up watching the soaps with my mom. On the soaps, life looks so easy. Someone blows into town penniless. A few months later, they're living in a luxury apartment. A few months after that, they're a company president or a doctor or a lawyer. But I find life to be really hard."

Carly thought for a moment. Then she slowly finished her sandwich and wiped her mouth with a napkin. She looked at me pointedly and said, "Let me tell you something, mister. I grew up watching the soaps with my mom. Life looked really easy to me, too, after watching all those soaps. Beautiful clothes. Nice cars. All those hunky guys. I find life to be really hard, also. All because of those fucking soaps. So, I have the exact goddamn problem. Never go to a psychologist who has the same problem as you. If you had issues with booze, drugs, sex, or food I could help you. But you don't seem to have those problems. So, I can't fucking help you. Have a nice day."

Exit: Carly, stage left.

EASTERN EUROPE AND SHIT

Oh, yeah. I almost forgot about my trip to Slovenia. I spent six months in Slovenia living with Mateuz and his parents. We had an import-export business marketing local foods to overseas distributers. Mostly, we were smuggling cigarettes. Or trying to. Except that I didn't know it was smuggling at the time. We would try to put together deals between cigarette buyers and sellers on the phone. Usually it amounted to a bunch of phone tag. We would call Saudi and get a four-year-old kid on the phone. When we asked for his dad, we'd hear a voice in the background saying, "Take care of business, Mohammed. You need to learn the business." Or some nutbag from overseas would call us at three in the morning and say, "It's nine in the morning at your local time, right? Let's do a deal." Or many freaks would call us and say they had one hundred million barrels of oil to sell. Very unlikely. Such a person might pull off a small deal concerning twenty thousand barrels of bunker (marine) fuel, if he wasn't such a clueless fuck.

One time we met some Italian mafia guys in the rain in a cemetery near the Italian border. When I was introduced to this elegant, older cat in a black cape, he got nose-to-nose with me and stared into my eyes for a full two minutes. If I hadn't been so drunk, I would have been scared shitless.

As for the country, it was beautiful. Lush, green rolling fields broken up by lovely, old villages with stone buildings. Ljubljana, the capital, had many lovely areas, like the three bridges area downtown, where a large collection of stately white architectural treasures from the time of Maria Theresa sat, when Slovenia was part of the Austro-Hungarian Empire.

We drove all over the country at one hundred and ten miles per hour, visiting Mateuz's many relatives. We visited really pretty cities like Marabor and really old ones like Ptuy, where we enjoyed hot mulled wine at a harvest festival that had been celebrated annually there since 1372. That harvest festival was pretty trippy. A bunch of guys there dressed up as corncobs and would surround young men and women and dry hump them.

We drove to parties that took place in these special party huts somewhere in the woods. Mateuz would turn off the highway into a clearing in the woods that would go on for miles. Then there would be forks in the road. Then we would drive for miles and take more forks in the road. Then we would get lost and take more forks in the road. The dirt roads were narrow, so we often had to stop and let the other car pass. This was scary at night, because you could barely sense the other car coming, and also, a lot of people drove with a snootful over there. Even the police drank beer on their breaks.

Anyway, after forty-five minutes of this Hansel and Gretel woods action, we found this twenty by twenty foot rustic hut in a clearing in the dark. It contained fifteen twenty-year-olds and about twenty-five bottles of hard liquor. Basically, the party consisted of everyone group groping everyone until the booze ran out the next day. I like the group hug part, but we bailed at the orgy thingy.

Mateuz's grandfather was a commander in the partisans during World War II. At one point in the war, the partisans requested military aid from the United States to bolster their valiant and successful defense of their country from the Germans. A few weeks later, the partisans were taken to a football-sized field with an enormous collection of tanks, jeeps, planes, rifles, grenade, and food. The partisans looked at this pile of military aid and thanked the American supply officers profusely.

"What aid? This ain't shit. It's just the samples. Tell us how much you want of each item."

The partisans cried in gratitude and disbelief.

One night we had dinner with a most interesting man. The intelligence chief under Tito. Mateuz's father had worked with him for many years. The party began at eight, but the food wasn't served until midnight. The first four hours were the cocktail session. Each guest was given four glasses, one for red wine, white wine, brandy, and beer. If one glass became empty, it was immediately refilled. Never try to keep up with Eastern Europeans in the drinking department.

That evening, the spymaster told me three most interesting things.

1. Hitler escaped. The spymaster said that he was in a meeting once with Tito and Stalin. At this meeting, Stalin declared that Hitler was never captured. Stalin said that Hitler escaped to South America. He also said that the "Hitler capture story" was a fairytale concocted by the Americans and the Brits to placate their citizens, who would have felt cheated if they knew the truth.

2. American POWS from the Vietnam War remained in Laos. The spymaster related a meeting with Andropov when he was head of the KGB. Andropov produced photos and witness testimony to confirm this fact. Andropov related that the North Vietnamese leaders told him of a deal that Nixon cut with them whereby Nixon would pay several billion dollars from a black-ops fund to help rebuild Vietnam in exchange for a peace treaty. According to the deal, the North Vietnamese would hold fifteen hundred American POWS as hostages until they received the money. However, Watergate arrived, and Nixon ended up with no dough to pay the North Vietnamese. And so, the North Vietnamese ended up keeping the POWS as hostages to save face. And to this day, the United States keeps denying the existence of American POWS in Vietnam and Laos.

3. Andropov also told the spymaster that there was extensive flying saucer activity going on in Antarctica. However, the KGB could not determine if the saucers were of alien origin, American, or a collaboration between the two.

In closing, the only thing I've really learned in life is to make a lot of friends and make a life list of things to do, and get on with it. Without friends, I would never have been so happy, and I would never have had so much fun. Plus, my health would have suffered, because as you remember, my pals saved my skin in several losing fistfights. By working on a to-do list, I mean that if one has a dream, and if he only takes one step in the direction of the dream, magic happens. That was the case with the writing of this mangy sheet.

It reminds me of one more story. In the early 1990s, I had the dream of starting a local radio show. Well, just a few weeks after signing up for a radio show at the local university, I received a phone call from this sweet, pudgy go-getter name Steve Schmid, who told me that we were paired by the station manager to begin a movie review show in two weeks. And a few weeks after that, Steve and I found ourselves having lunch with Renée Zellweger as we interviewed her about her latest movie.

Renée was really friendly, witty, and sharp. She said that the people who wasted their lives working at jobs they hated were retards. She also said that several of these retards used to haze her when she was growing up in a trailer park in Texas. She advised Steve and me, as tender, fat youths, to not waste our lives doing shit we hated just to buy a bunch of junk in a ham-handed attempt to impress the retards. Well said.

Anyway, this old Mac computer is really starting to die now. I would like to tell you guys about my trip to Dubai with Mateuz. I'd like to tell about the great food, like the fragrant pilaf dishes with grilled meats. About the swanky five-star hotel we stayed in for only eighty dollars per night, because the second Gulf War had just started, and all the Westerners were pussing out. And how the owner of one restaurant snuck a skewer of grilled brains on my plate. (Looks like pineapple, tastes like chicken.) And how one corner-shop owner got angry that I was American when I tried to buy a phone card there and pulled out a Koran and started reading, as his friends yelled, "Ali, no, be calm. Be calm!" And I'd like to talk about the beautiful modern buildings that look like expensive cigarette lighters. And the old covered mall souks where they sell expensive, exotic perfume and gold and silks. And I need to mention the funky old shopping areas with the neon signs and the clothing racks full of exotic gear spilling onto the sidewalks. Where Mateuz's dad, Branco, (who is a dead ringer for Joseph Stalin) spent days trying on exotic silk robes, turbans, and pointy slippers, and chatting up the beautiful shopgirls in Russian. But I'll talk about such trips in another volume.

Bye for now,
That's Dee, Brother.

Made in the USA
Monee, IL
07 July 2026

56552674R00080